Tort, Custom, and Karma

THE CULTURAL LIVES OF LAW
Edited by Austin Sarat

Tort, Custom, and Karma

Globalization and Legal Consciousness in Thailand

David M. Engel and Jaruwan S. Engel

Stanford Law Books
An Imprint of Stanford University Press
Stanford, California

Stanford University Press
Stanford, California

Printed in the United States of America on acid-free, archival-quality paper

Library of Congress Cataloging-in-Publication Data

Engel, David M.
    Tort, custom, and karma : globalization and legal consciousness in Thailand / David M. Engel and Jaruwan S. Engel.
        p. cm—(The cultural lives of law)
    Includes bibliographical references and index.
    ISBN 978-0-8047-6381-3 (cloth : alk. paper)—ISBN 978-0-8047-6382-0 (pbk. : alk. paper)
    1. Torts—Thailand. 2. Law and globalization—Thailand. 3. Buddhism and law—Thailand. 4. Culture and law. I. Engel, Jaruwan S. II. Title. III. Series: Cultural lives of law. KPT834.E545 2010
    346.59303—dc22
                        2009035121

Typeset by Thompson Type in 11/13.5 Adobe Garamond

To the memory of Kanyamas Saiprasert, nong rak,
and to our children, Anya and Mark

Contents

Illustrations

Acknowledgments

OUR RESEARCH ON INJURIES AND LAW in northern Thailand began in 1975 when we were introduced to Chiangmai and the north by Ms. Kanyamas Saiprasert, to whose memory this book is dedicated. We were already familiar with other regions: One of us had worked for three years as an educator in southern Thailand, and the other was born and raised in central Thailand. But with our sister we began to explore and came to love the Lanna region, its history, and its people. Our research yielded a monograph about law and society in Thailand (Engel 1978). Circumstances then prevented us from returning to Thailand for many years, but in 1990 we were able to resume our visits and, eventually, to launch the research project that gave rise to this book. Our fifteen-year absence from Thailand, though unfortunate in many ways, did have the advantage of making unmistakably clear to us how Thai society had changed during this crucially important period in its history. These changes ultimately became the central theme of our restudy of legal culture in Chiangmai a quarter of a century after our first effort. Of course we had no way of knowing when we began our research that the dramatic social transformations in Thailand had led to a counterintuitive decline in the role of law in injury cases. One of the great pleasures of empirical research is its endless capacity to surprise.

As a result of our increasingly frequent and lengthy stays in Chiangmai during the 1990s, we developed close cooperative relationships with colleagues at Chiang Mai University, and we also had the opportunity to teach a number of students at the CMU Law School. We consider ourselves blessed by these contacts and friendships and by the chance to learn from such a talented and dedicated group of scholars and students.

It is impossible to list the names of all our friends and colleagues at CMU, but we must single out a few for special mention. Dr. Kobkun Rayanakorn and her remarkable family provided unstinting support, encouragement, and insight along with her warmth and hospitality. Dr. Nidhi Eoseewong has offered us his friendship, advice, and intellectual counsel for more than three decades. Ajan Virada Somswasdi and Ajan Shalardchai Ramitanon provided wisdom and direction as well as delicious home-cooked meals and memorable conversation. Our friends Dr. Panarairat Srichaiyarat and Ajan Kanya Hirunwattanapong generously helped us to launch our fieldwork and to engage and supervise student research assistants. Dean Chatree Ruangdetnarong was an unfailing source of support, encouragement, and counsel, and it has been a special pleasure for us to have become close to him and his delightful family. We deeply appreciate the friendship and support of CMU Vice President Pong-In Rakariyatham. Several other friends and colleagues at CMU directly contributed to or participated in our research: Ajan Paisit Panichakul, Ajan Nuthamon Kongcharoen, Ajan Somchai Preechasilpakul, Ajan Watis Sotthibandhu, Dr. Anan Ganjanapan, and Ajan Ekamol Saichan. We thank all of them for their invaluable help and advice. Khun Thawee Khunyotying provided a unique introduction to the culture and landscape of Lanna, and we are grateful for his guidance and his many stories and insights.

Funding for this study was provided by the National Science Foundation, grant no. SBR98-10372, and by the Baldy Center for Law and Social Policy at the University at Buffalo, State University of New York. We have received excellent support from a number of able and dedicated research assistants. Three individuals played a key role in our Chiangmai-based fieldwork, and we are grateful for their many outstanding contributions: Duen Wongsa, Sutthira Foocom, and Rotjarek Intachote. Another group of research assistants worked diligently and thoughtfully for us in Buffalo: Joshua Dilk, Usa Gopal, John Hannibal, Wipha Iamsamang, Sarah Kim, Suda Rangkupan, Viliporn Runkawatt, and Warit Silavisesrith. Thanks as always go to Dawn Fenneman for her many contributions to our work.

Many other friends and colleagues have offered suggestions and encouragement, listened to numerous presentations of our work, and read and critiqued various drafts. Although it is impossible to list all their names, we want to single out just a few for special thanks: Irus Braverman, David Chambers, Roger Des Forges, Howard Erlanger, Rebecca French, Bruce Jackson, Robert Kidder, Takanori Kitamura, Alfred Konefsky, Lynn Mather, Michael McCann, Frank Munger, Frank Reynolds, Austin Sarat, Winnifred Sullivan, and Barbara Yngvesson. Anya Engel carefully read the entire manuscript and offered many cogent and extremely helpful suggestions. We would like to thank Nayada Jirampaikool for her help in preparing many of the photographs that appear in this book. Thanks to Patrick Whitaker for taking two of the photographs at our request. Thanks also to Jessie Poon for helping with the figures that display our litigation data.

We thank the administrators and staff of the Chiangmai Provincial Court for facilitating our extended study of case records. We thank the administrators of the Suan Dok Hospital for providing space and support that enabled us to conduct our interviews with injury victims.

We owe a profound debt of gratitude to the injury victims who gave their time and insights so generously during the extended interviews that form the core of this study. When we began our research, we did not realize how extraordinarily rich these injury narratives would be, nor did we imagine that they would illuminate so extensively the history and culture of the Lanna region. We were deeply moved by these accounts and soon recognized that they provided unique insights into Chiangmai's past and present as well as the life histories of individuals who have contended with painful challenges during a time of dramatic social change. In writing this book, we have been conscious of our obligation to convey these stories sensitively and accurately and to make them understandable to readers who may be unfamiliar with Thailand. We thank all of the interviewees for making this book possible.

Our family cheerfully put up with our travels and our seemingly endless journeys to villages and temples throughout northern Thailand, and they even joined us in some of our excursions. For their patience and understanding we are truly grateful. We can only hope that this remarkable region we have come to love will continue to enrich the lives of our children as it has enriched our own.

Note on Romanization
of Thai Words and Phrases

ALL THAI WORDS AND PHRASES in this book appear in italics. We have used the Royal Thai General System of Transcription, published by the Royal Institute of Thailand, to romanize Thai expressions, although we have introduced a few minor exceptions for the benefit of readers unfamiliar with Thai pronunciation. Instead of the RTGST vowel *ue*, we use *ŭ*, resulting in *mŭang* rather than *mueang*. The RTGST does not distinguish between the aspirated and unaspirated forms of *ch*, but we render the unaspirated form as *j*, producing *thammajak* rather than *thammachak*. For words and names that have acquired a familiar romanized form, such as *baht* or *Chulalongkorn*, we have retained that form rather than applying our version of the RTGST to make them *bat* and *Julalongkon*. Similarly, we have not changed the romanization of proper names that individuals have transliterated themselves, nor have we altered the romanization of words and phrases in quoted material.

Readers not familiar with the Thai language should note that in transcription systems such as the RTGST, *h* is commonly used to indicate an aspirated consonant. Thus, *ph* sounds like the *p* in the English word *pin,* and *p* sounds like the unaspirated *p* in *spin*. *Th* sounds like the *t* in the English word *top*, and *t* sounds like the unaspirated *t* in *stop*. Similarly, *kh* sounds like the *k* in the English word *kin*, while *k* sounds like the unaspirated *k* in *skin*.

Unfortunately, the RTGST does not permit a distinction between the closed and open *o* vowels, which are both transcribed as *o*, nor does it distinguish between long and short Thai vowels or indicate tones. Nevertheless, the virtue of the RTGST is that it has become a widely accepted standard, and the absence of exotic symbols makes it relatively readable.

Introduction

Inta's Injury Narrative

The economic boom of the 1990s brought a young man named Inta[1] from the rice fields of northern Thailand to a factory near the city, where he operated a stamping machine making cardboard boxes. It was dangerous work and paid just 144 *baht* (about $3.60) per day. The brake on the stamping machine didn't function properly, and other employees had already been injured. No one, not even Inta, was surprised when one day his hand was caught in the machine and mangled beyond repair. What may be surprising, however, is the explanation he offers for the horrifying injury and his assumption about who—or what—was responsible.

Inta's injury narrative does not characterize his employer as irresponsible or greedy. In fact, he never blames his employer at all, nor does he attribute fault to the manufacturer of the defective stamping machine. Instead, he asserts that the primary causes of his injury were a ghost and his own karma. As Inta tells the story, he was riding to work one day on his motorcycle when he came on a group of villagers at the scene of an accident. He stopped to see what had happened and observed a shocking sight: the corpse of a man who had just driven his motorcycle into a banana tree and broken his neck. Inta learned that two other unnatural deaths (*tai hong*) had occurred in the past at this very spot, one by drowning and the other by stabbing. It was clearly a dangerous and haunted location.

Inta continued on his way to the factory that day, and for the next five months he drove past the accident site as he traveled to and from work. Each time, he could not help thinking about the dead man he had seen there. Later, a spirit medium revealed to Inta's mother that this man's ghost had caused Inta's injury. By allowing the dead person to enter his thoughts, Inta had made himself vulnerable to the ghost's influence, and its chance finally came while Inta was working at the factory. One day Inta felt the ghost push on his shoulder to extend his arm, and he felt it pull the fingers of his hand into the stamping machine, where they were crushed. Because Inta sensed the ghost's intervention so strongly, he did not question the spirit medium's causal explanation. As soon as he made an offering to the ghost, the swelling in his arm disappeared, which Inta took as confirmation of its role in his injury.

It was a pity that Inta had failed to present the offering before he was injured, for he had been keenly aware of the ghost's presence. He felt light headed each time he drove past that location near the highway. Inta could have performed a ceremony to make merit for the soul of the man who had died there. Had he done so, his own accident might never have happened. He had been forewarned, but he had done nothing. Furthermore, Inta's own karma was probably at low ebb. That was why the ghost had selected him out of all those who passed by. Inta had failed to present offerings in the temple or perform other virtuous acts that would have strengthened his karma and protected him against misfortune. In the end, Inta realized that he had brought the injury on himself.

Inta's explanation of the injury makes it highly unlikely that he would perceive his accident as the result of someone else's wrongdoing. His short-term medical treatment was covered by workers' compensation insurance, and he received half his salary during a portion of his convalescence. Nevertheless, Inta experienced a great deal of uncompensated pain and suffering. He lost a substantial amount of income during and after convalescence, and his future employment prospects are bleak; but Inta feels his boss has treated him with kindness. The accident was his own fault, and to demand further payment from the maker of the machine, his employer, or anyone else could only worsen Inta's karmic imbalance and lead to greater misfortune. Should he consider whether the law might entitle him to further help with his personal and financial setbacks? The question never occurs to him.

Globalization and Law in the Lives of Ordinary People

What happens to law in the lives of ordinary people when a society undergoes rapid change, economic development, and integration into global markets? It is said that the world has become compressed, flattened, and interdependent. Diverse societies are now connected by transnational cultural, economic, and demographic forces propelled across continents by new communication technologies and massive flows of information, people, goods, and capital. What happens, in such circumstances, to popular perceptions of the law and to the readiness of ordinary people to make use of legal ideas, norms, and institutions? Is it accurate to say that inherent in the globalization process is a heightened consciousness of the rule of law and an increased willingness to mobilize it rather than to interpret experience in terms of other discourses or meaning systems that make official law less relevant or even invisible? In short, what is the *legal consciousness*[2] of ordinary people as they cope from day to day with a transformed world?

The conventional answer to this question is that the embrace of "liberal legalism" is a central feature of globalization. Liberal legalism, though variously conceived in different societies and world regions, includes some commitment to rule of law practices and institutions, individual rights, free markets, and democratic government. As peoples, cultures, and markets become increasingly interconnected, certain aspects of liberal legalism are considered by its proponents to be not only attractive ideals but also practical necessities. During times of dislocation and change, liberal legal regimes provide a universal discourse that defines obligations, relationships, and actors. They offer an institutional and procedural framework that facilitates transactions across cultural and social boundaries. It is said that rule of law concepts and practices, viewed initially as mechanisms to promote the expansion of an international market economy, tend inevitably to spill over into other nonmarket areas of social life where they fundamentally change interactions and expectations:

> [O]ver time, there is likely to be spillover from the commercial area into other areas such as family law, environmental law, criminal law and administrative law. A legal system that is able to deliver competent, efficient, fair decisions in economic cases requires certain institutions and norms among the judiciary and state actors, as well as an investment in their professionalization and legal training. Such reforms, however, tend to take on a life of their own as institutions evolve and seek to expand their authority, as judges and other state actors begin to internalize professional norms, and as citizens come to expect judges and administrative officials to ensure that the government lives up to its commitment to rule of law. (Peerenboom 2004, 39–40)

According to this view, globalization "accentuates individualism, and increases resort to law for the affirmation of individual rights" (Pérez-Perdomo and Friedman 2003, 5). Globalization transforms the consciousness of ordinary people and creates new expectations about the place of law, legal norms, and legal institutions in their lives.

It is not clear, however, whether this theoretical relationship between globalization and liberal legalism actually becomes manifest in the everyday lives and legal consciousness of ordinary people. Indeed, some observers have contended that globalization can have the opposite effect, that it produces a backlash, that its liberal and promarket ideology creates disaffection among those who fail to benefit or who actively resist the expansion of global capitalism. The backlash, according to this view, leads to a rejection of legal liberalism in favor of other ideologies, such as religious fundamentalism. Segments of the population may come to embrace traditional religious rules, procedures, and institutions rather than secular legality. This tendency may be particularly strong among minorities and among majority groups who have lost out during the social and economic transformations (Chua 2002). Globalization, in short, may trigger a legal "spirit" quite different from that envisioned by Enlightenment philosophers (Montesquieu 1989 [1748]); it could be associated with the rise of antiliberal and, indeed, antimodern concepts of justice. In this book, we embrace neither the more expansive view nor its antithesis. Instead of seeking to identify a singular direct or inverse relationship between globalization and liberal legalism, we think it useful to ask how globalization may affect key elements of legal culture and consciousness, each of which has significance for the role of law in the lives of ordinary people. In our research, five such elements have emerged with dramatic clarity from the narratives of numerous men and women who, like Inta, suffered serious injuries. Our analysis of law in northern Thailand will therefore examine with particular care the relationship of globalization to the following:

1. *Spatial and temporal frameworks.* Sassen (2001, 260), writing of the processes associated with globalization, has observed, "Among the most vital of their effects is the production of new spatialities and temporalities." Law requires and operates within distinct conceptions of time and space. As these conceptions change, we should expect fundamental shifts in popular understandings of legal institutions and practices.

2. *Concepts of the self.* Identities and roles change as individuals participate directly or indirectly in social, economic, and cultural processes on a global scale. In the Thai context, we will see transformations in such key components of personhood as mind, body, identity, spirit, and soul. Law is constituted by the activities of human (and sometimes those of supernatural) actors. With changes in the actors' essential attributes, the laws that regulate them may also change, may be used in new ways, or may be abandoned.

3. *Community, social networks, and relationships.* Social and economic changes can weaken traditional communities and social networks and can loosen the ties between individuals and their birth communities. Individuals may find themselves in new kinds of social relationships or may experience greater social isolation than before. These new relationships and interactions may require—and produce—new forms of law.

4. *Justice norms and procedures.* New types of social relationship and interaction may be associated with new ideas about justice and how to achieve it. Unprecedented global information flows can communicate new concepts of justice from distant regions of the world, making it possible to raise novel questions about existing legal systems and the degree to which they provide justice or fail to do so.

5. *Cosmology and religious belief.* The effects of globalization have been associated with new religious practices and beliefs, although in various and sometimes unpredictable forms. Both secularism and fundamentalism have been identified as the inevitable products of globalization. In the Thai context, the vast majority of the population is Buddhist, and Buddhism is central to the legitimacy of the Thai state (Reynolds 1994). We shall closely examine the changes that have occurred in Buddhism and its relationship to spirit worship—and their implications for law.

We shall have more to say on the topic of globalization in Chapter 2, where we discuss the meaning(s) of the term and its relevance to our research site: the province of Chiangmai in northern Thailand. For now, suffice it to say that our purpose is not to suggest a simple theory of cause and effect or to view globalization merely as an independent variable acting on culture and consciousness. Rather, we ask to what extent globalization tends to be accompanied by particular kinds of change in these five aspects of legal culture and to what extent such changes make it easier for global influences to take root in society.

We have conducted fieldwork in Thailand over a thirty-year span during which global forces became particularly intense. Drawing primarily on our ethnographic interviews with people in the province of Chiangmai who suffered serious injuries and on records of injury cases in the Chiangmai Provincial Court, we will examine the connections between globalization and new forms of legal consciousness. We will conclude that a transformation in the legal consciousness of individual citizens has indeed occurred, but it has led neither to a heightened commitment to rule of law ideology nor to a rejection of the norms and values of a market economy. Instead, law in all its forms appears to have diminished in importance. Although new kinds of religiosity now predominate in the lives of most injury victims, they lead to acceptance and forgiveness of wrongdoing in place of a quest for compensation. With globalization has come the disappearance of legal remedies. Injury victims such as Inta do not search for a mechanism by which they could hold another person responsible, nor do they view the misdeeds of someone else as the root of the problem. Injured persons rarely if ever conceive of their experiences in legal terms or pursue legal claims.

As we trace the changes that have produced this surprising transformation in the role of law, we will describe a fundamental shift in the interconnections between state law and customary practices. As we discuss in Chapter 3, sociolegal theorists from Weber to the present have postulated that state law derives meanings, legitimacy, and authority from its relationship to systems of nonstate legality. In Thailand, the most familiar nonstate legal orders are village based and draw on widely shared conceptions of community, personhood, and locality-based norms and practices. The global changes Thailand has experienced during the last three decades have disrupted village communities and weakened customary practices for handling injuries. As a result, the relationship between state law and nonstate law has changed.

Although one might have expected that state law would increase in importance as nonstate law declines, we have found that *both* state and nonstate law have become less salient for those who suffer physical injuries. Their accounts provide little evidence that the spirit of liberal legalism has expanded and taken root in the consciousness of ordinary people during the recent era of global change. On the contrary, the transformation of the landscape of injuries has left Thai people bereft of any form of law and without any workable remedy when they suffer harm at the hands of another person.

Personal Injuries and the Study of Late Twentieth-Century Social Change

It might seem odd to focus on personal injuries[3] to explore the relationship between law and global change. Usually scholars interested in these questions choose to study international trade, human rights, the legal profession, the environment, or even constitutional or administrative law. Torts and tort law have not been the site of much scholarly activity among students of globalization.[4] The typical Thai case of injury caused by careless driving or a sporting mishap may seem remote from and irrelevant to the world of multinational corporations, nongovernmental organizations (NGOs), and international lawyers. Yet it is precisely this remoteness that makes the injury narratives of ordinary people such a valuable subject for inquiry. In these accounts we can see with remarkable clarity how new information flows, new economic arrangements and activities, new patterns of internal migration, and new ideologies and belief systems create new human identities and new perceptions about the self and the community and about social practices and responsibilities. In these stories, with their immediacy, intimacy, pain, and beauty, we can perceive quite clearly how law and justice recede from the grasp of ordinary people even as they seek a vocabulary to express their sense of loss.

Activities that are most consonant with Western liberal legalism tend to catch the eye of Western observers, who may have little opportunity to assess directly the legal consciousness of ordinary Thai citizens. If we look for Coca-Cola signs in other societies, we will certainly find them; but that does not necessarily mean that ordinary people there have adopted the ways of thinking and behaving that are associated with "Coca-Colonization." To discover whether that sort of transformation has occurred, we must go beyond highly familiar (to us) and readily visible signs and find other ways to understand the changes and continuities of everyday life.

Similarly, because American and European sociolegal scholars often undertake studies that search for familiar (to them) institutions or practices that reflect their own preconceptions of law and legal change, they tend to engage in self-fulfilling prophecy and make findings that closely match their presuppositions about the effects of globalization. As Tsing (2002, 476) has observed, "In globalization theories, we have confused what should be *questions* about the global ramifications of new technologies and social processes with *answers* about global change." Sociolegal scholars have tended to find what they are looking for and, consequently, to draw exaggerated conclusions about the impact of European and American legal ideologies on Thai society or, for that matter, on societies throughout the world. The relevant actors in their studies tend to be members of the social elite, often Western or Western educated and steeped in the liberal legal tradition. Although this type of research may examine instances of localized resistance to global power and may point to the emergence of new sociolegal spaces and fields within the global order, its primary interest is in the movement of ideas and actors from what is conceived as the center outward and from the top downward. From this perspective, analysts often highlight the pervasiveness of American and European influences but less often provide insight into the thoughts and experiences of ordinary people at ground level.

By contrast, our study associates itself with research that asks a different question about law and recent global changes: How have the "time-space compression" (Harvey 1990, 240) and the "global cultural flows" (Appadurai 1996) interacted with the legal consciousness and everyday practices of ordinary people and the role law plays in their social dealings?[5] We ask to what extent the "internal coherence" of the ideology of rights and liberal legalism has been preserved or "loosened" as the cultural waves of globalization have washed across Chiangmai's social landscape (Appadurai 1996, 36).

We chose, then, not to study the activities of Western-educated legal elites or of organizations that deliberately try to propagate liberal legalism in Thailand. Such studies may have great value, but they cannot answer the question we wanted to ask: What changes, if any, have occurred in the conceptions of law, legal institutions, and justice among ordinary Thai people during a time of social transformation linked to sweeping global influences? Personal injuries offer several advantages as a field in which to explore these issues. First, injuries are very often the by-products of rapid social change. We anticipated at the outset of this study that several decades of globalization in Thailand would have increased the frequency and possibly the severity of injuries. By studying how injuries were handled, we hoped to shed light on the interconnections between globalization and law.

Second, mechanisms for handling injuries can be found at many levels and locations in Thailand, making them a particularly rich subject for study. Although tort law is one means to address the problem of injury, there are others that have little if any connection to the official legal system. The demand for compensation by injured persons is neither new to Thai society nor is it associated exclusively with law courts or liberal legal ideology. In Thai village society there has for centuries been an extensive customary law that required injurers to pay compensation to their victims. Modern Thai tort law emerged with clarity in 1935 with the promulgation of the Thai Civil and Commercial Code, long before the time period covered by our research. The broad array of options, concepts, and beliefs concerning injuries in Thailand is a great advantage in a study that aims to explore the connections between recent global changes and the legal consciousness of ordinary people. It enables us to examine and compare the entire range of responses by injury victims, not just those that are obviously associated with liberal legalism but also those that have existed for centuries and those with little apparent connection to the law. By focusing on the problem of injuries in its many social manifestations, we can avoid building a rule-of-law or "presentist" bias into our inquiry from the outset. We have tried not to design our study in a way that will inevitably lead to the conclusion that global legal actors, ideas, and institutions are on the ascendancy in Thailand.

The study of personal injuries offers a third advantage: It tells us a great deal about fundamental conceptions of self and society. Personal injuries are just that—injuries of the *person*. The perception that such an injury has occurred rests on a set of assumptions about what a person is; what aspects of the person can be harmed; what connections exist between harms to the body, the personality, and the network of social relationships; and what measures can and should be taken to repair the harm that an injury causes and thereby restore the person to her or his place in society. Tanabe (2002) observes that in the past personhood in northern Thai culture was unstable and lacked "solid boundaries." He suggests that social and economic transformations of the late twentieth century brought pressure on these longstanding conceptions of the permeable and interconnected human personality and rendered them problematic, giving rise to new kinds of beliefs and practices. The study of personal injuries can illuminate cultural shifts of this kind, especially during periods of industrialization or rapid social change. If the human personality is now perceived in more bounded and individuated terms, it may be apparent in the way people perceive injuries and respond to them.

Whether and to what extent law becomes a part of such transformations in the concept of personhood is therefore a question of great importance as we seek to understand the changes globalization has brought to the lives and legal consciousness of ordinary people.

Finally, the study of personal injuries provides a particularly useful window onto law and social change because personal injuries are closely connected to a constellation of concepts that have fundamental importance for the role of law. One such concept is causation. A remarkable feature of the injury narratives we present in this book is the multiplicity of causes each of them cites. We will suggest that each causal frame corresponds to a different cluster of beliefs about self, society, and the supernatural. A second concept is compensation. What is it that must be paid when a person is injured and to whom? On what scale and by what currency are injuries to be valued? Ideas about compensation are likely to change with transformations of human identity and with the expansion of capitalism and a cash economy. A third concept is justice. As we will suggest later in this book, discussions of personal injury cases lead naturally to broader reflections on what is just and fair. Such reflections reveal deep connections to religious thought and point to a growing divide between law and religion in contemporary Thailand.

Research Design and Methodology

Our fieldwork had two major components: (1) extended ethnographic interviews with more than a hundred individuals in Chiangmai, Thailand, thirty-five of whom had been hospitalized for treatment of serious injuries; and (2) a survey of personal injury and other tort cases litigated in the local trial court over a thirty-five-year period. In Chapter 2, we will describe Chiangmai's history in greater detail and will provide an overview of the dramatic changes it has recently experienced. Here we simply note that Chiangmai is generally considered the cultural and economic hub of the northern Thai region, and the city of Chiangmai is in many respects the most important urban area in Thailand outside of Bangkok.

The design of the study reflects a pyramid model of litigation and dispute processing that is familiar to and widely used by sociolegal scholars (see, e.g., Trubek et al. 1983). As applied to the personal injury field, the pyramid is said to rest on a broad base consisting of all the harms that might potentially be perceived as wrongful and, in some cases, as having legal significance. The middle layers of the injury pyramid involve unilateral or bilateral claims and negotiations, intervention by unofficial third party intermediaries or lawyers, and other extrajudicial settlement procedures. The tip of the pyramid involves tort cases that are actually litigated, adjudicated, and—even more rarely—appealed. Our study of injuries in Thailand concentrates on two layers of the pyramid: the base and the tip.

Saks (1992) provides perhaps the most detailed explication of the pyramid model in the context of the American tort law system. One of Saks's most important insights is that the characteristics of the pyramid's base must be understood before meaningful inferences can be drawn about any other aspect of the handling of tort cases in society. Analysis of "lumping," negotiation, settlement, or the decision to litigate depends on information about the pyramid's base: the number and kinds of injuries that occur in society and the ways in which individuals interpret them—the raw materials from which claims, disputes, or lawsuits might be fashioned (see generally Engel and Steele 1979; Mather and Yngvesson 1980–1981; Felstiner, Abel, and Sarat 1980–1981).

Understanding the base of the injury pyramid is thus essential to the analysis of all the other layers, including the litigation of tort cases. The perception and interpretation of injury determines all that follows—whether the injured person holds another party responsible, whether compensation is expected or demanded, what mechanisms for obtaining compensation are considered, and whether legal or other normative systems are invoked to assess the responsibilities of the parties. At the base of the pyramid, cultural factors are extraordinarily important. Here the analysis of legal consciousness can shed considerable light.

Our methodology for exploring the legal consciousness of ordinary people at the base of the injury pyramid in Chiangmai builds on research that examines how individuals tell stories about their lives, their experiences, their social relationships and interactions, and their sense of self. Such narratives are used primarily to understand the subjectivity of the narrators—how they interpret events, how they explain their own behavior and that of others, and how they view themselves in relation to the world around them and in relation to legal norms, procedures, and institutions. We encouraged interviewees to provide an extended narrative covering a broad sweep of time, in which they described their lives from childhood to present and the changes that had occurred in their social environment over a period of many years (comparable to the methodology in Engel and Munger 2003). Within the broader narrative of their personal history, they located the specific incident that caused them to seek treatment in a hospital for physical harm.

To obtain the injury narratives of ordinary people in Chiangmai, we identified a large hospital that treated patients from the entire province of Chiangmai and thus drew cases from a "jurisdiction" comparable to that of the provincial court. With the help of the staff at Suan Dok Hospital, we obtained the names of ninety-three current or recently discharged patients who had volunteered to participate in interviews. All had suffered physical injuries involving the conduct of another party.[6] After recording baseline data for all ninety-three volunteers, we selected thirty-five for extensive, in-depth interviews, which we conducted in Thai at the hospital or at the interviewee's home or place of work in 1999.[7] Participants were chosen to provide a range of perspectives, based primarily on rural versus urban background, gender, circumstances of the injury, and age.[8] Despite its diversity, this group was not a random sample of Chiangmai's population. The thirty-five interviewees were not selected to make quantitative predictions about a broader universe, but they do illustrate in considerable depth some of the ways in which globalization has affected the legal consciousness of differently situated individuals in Chiangmai.

This study focuses on the subjective and interpretive processes that occur in the pyramid's base, but the findings have implications for each succeeding level of the pyramid, including the use of courts and lawyers. While a systematic study of the entire injury pyramid in Thailand was beyond the scope of this study—and unfortunately there are few other studies of the injury pyramid in Thailand—we sought to shed additional light on the injury narratives by interviewing a number of other persons who had knowledge of injuries, village life, insurance, negotiations, legal practice, and other matters relevant to our study. Our study therefore included more than sixty-five additional interviews with a broad spectrum of persons ranging from village leaders to insurance adjusters, monks, spirit mediums, attorneys, judges, Thai scholars, doctors, government officials, and others. These interviews supplemented the thirty-five interviews with injury victims.

The second major component of the study, in addition to the interviews described above, consisted of an exploration of the tip of the injury pyramid—the Chiangmai Provincial Court. We had the great advantage of having researched tort litigation in the same court twenty-five years earlier. From 1974 to 1978, we had surveyed all the case files in the Chiangmai Provincial Court for cases litigated from 1965 through 1974. In particular, we obtained detailed information from the pleadings, witness testimony, and judicial opinions of every tort case that appeared in the court during four of those years: 1965, 1968, 1971, and 1974 (see Engel 1978). Further, we had conducted interviews in 1975 with litigants, lawyers, judges, police officers, village leaders, and others. Our study in the late 1990s was, in some respects, a "restudy" that involved a return to a familiar setting and provided an opportunity to trace changes and continuities over a relatively long period of time.

From 1997 to 2000 we once again surveyed the docket of the Chiangmai Provincial Court, this time selecting cases litigated from 1992 through 1997. Using the court registers, we identified every injury case filed by a private party. Most took the form of civil actions, but some were litigated as private criminal cases.[9] We retrieved and photocopied the entire case file of each of these civil and criminal cases, analyzed their contents, and compared them to the ten years of cases we had studied during our previous fieldwork in 1975. As we shall discuss in later chapters of this book, we found to our surprise that tort litigation rates at the tip of the injury pyramid had actually decreased over the past quarter-century, and this finding proved to be consistent with the alienation from law we discovered at the base of the injury pyramid. These parallel developments at different levels of the pyramid invite more general theorizing about the relationships among globalization, legal consciousness, and tort law in Thailand. Therefore, although much of this book focuses on the injury narratives, we analyze them with one eye on the diminished rate of litigation in the formal legal system, and we suggest that both the base and the tip of the pyramid reflect and contribute to the social transformations Chiangmai has experienced during the past twenty-five years.

Injury Narratives: Their Form and Function

This book begins and ends with fully rendered injury narratives. The first, which appears in Chapter 1, is the story told to us by "Buajan," the pseudonym of a middle-aged woman whose leg was severely injured when a person she describes as an "old man" ran her down with his car. Buajan's narrative provides the perspective of a generation born into the practices and belief systems of northern Thai villagers. She, however, like others of her generation, left her birth community to work in the city. Buajan retains many of the beliefs instilled by her parents and grand-parents, but she lives far from the "sacred centers" where such beliefs are put into practice. Her injury narrative reveals how a person with strong religious beliefs must now contend with the changed circumstances of contemporary life. Her story reflects the intersection of globalization with long-standing practices and beliefs about persons, injuries, responsibility, and remediation.

The second injury narrative, which appears in Chapter 7, is an account by "Ming," a young man who repairs power lines for an electrical contractor. By contrast with Buajan, Ming's injury narrative offers insight into the perspective of a self-styled member of the "new generation." He has only a superficial awareness of traditional beliefs and practices and frequently insists that he rejects them. He is impatient with references to ghosts, spirits, and even Buddhism and dismisses them as the outmoded views of an older generation. Yet in Ming's narrative we can clearly see some continuities with the past. He acknowledges the importance of customary practices to ensure good luck and to propitiate locality spirits on some occasions, and he even ascribes a serious injury to the wrath of a locality spirit whom he inadvertently offended. Ming's injury narrative thus provides a strong sense of the future in northern Thailand: retaining some features of customary beliefs and practices but without any connection to the remediation mechanisms that might formerly have provided him with compensation when he was injured. His narrative also expresses strong skepticism about the potential of the Thai legal system to grant justice to ordinary people like himself.

The bookend injury narratives of Buajan and Ming are key to our presentation. They provide the reader with a more complete version of the interviewee perspectives that we cite in briefer excerpts throughout the book. By reading these contrasting generational narratives, the reader will be able to understand the materials on which we have relied in writing this book and will gain firsthand exposure to the expressions and viewpoints of two representative interviewees. In addition, the presentation of these two injury narratives underscores our commitment to a particular type of research. When conducting fieldwork about matters of consciousness, perception, and interpretation, we considered it unproductive for our purposes to formulate close-ended survey questions about fundamental concepts such as injury, law, obligation, and justice. We will explain in later chapters of this book why such concepts are difficult to translate into Thai and why certain types of questions about them could be potentially confusing or even irrelevant to our interviewees.

We found it most productive, speaking in Thai with our interviewees,[10] to ask them to tell us their stories in their own words, beginning with childhood memories and continuing through various adult experiences to the injury that brought them to the hospital for treatment (compare Engel and Munger 2003). Because they recited narratives that described broad expanses of time and experience, our interviewees were able to frame matters in words and categories of their own choosing and to tell us about their injuries in a vocabulary that made sense to them. We listened carefully to the words and ideas they volunteered as they told their stories. We waited to see if and when they might introduce liberal legal concepts of rights, process, or justice. Because few of them did so, we ourselves eventually asked about these concepts and their meanings—but only after the interviewees had concluded their own narrative accounts.

The injury narratives, because of the way in which they were recounted, had a built-in longitudinal dimension. We did not actually follow our interviewees over time, but they described to us what the passage of time had meant for them and what changes they had experienced as Thailand underwent a series of dramatic socioeconomic transformations in the later part of the twentieth century. Thus, our research did have an important temporal dimension, and the childhood memories of our interviewees became a central feature of our data. The contrasts they drew between their own beliefs and practices and those of their parents and grandparents were highly important to us in our analysis of the transformations associated with globalization.

Of course, we were not able to verify the truthfulness or accuracy of each of these narratives. Our analyses do not rest on an assumption that the stories the interviewees told were in accord with some objective reality, whatever that term might mean in this context (for example, did the ghost really cause Inta's injury?). The primary value of narrative-based research is that it can demonstrate how individuals perceive themselves and their experiences in relation to broader systems of belief or social practice. Although the "facts" recounted in these narratives may be of great importance to the narrator, this type of research does not necessarily seek external confirmation that events occurred as described, nor does it compare rival interpretations. The subjectivity of the narrator—in this case the interpretation offered by the injured person—is the object of study. The contrasts our interviewees drew between past and present, "there" and "here," others and themselves, justice and injustice, were precisely what we hoped to learn from them. We could not say whether a particular story of fairness or unfairness would have been told the same way by the other parties involved (or by a third-party observer), but we could say with some confidence that it revealed the categories, concepts, and beliefs that had great significance for its narrator.

Moreover, we consider the very act of telling these stories to be an important social event. An injury narrative is an exercise in meaning creation. It defines what has happened in terms that the narrator wants others to understand and to believe. The desire and intention of the narrator is important for researchers to recognize. Each story is an attempt to persuade the listener to accept a particular version of reality. Further, the narrative not only defines events and their meanings, it also creates identities. It answers the question of who the narrator is and who are the people with whom she or he has interacted. Narrative and identity are thus inextricably linked (see generally Bruner 1990; Amsterdam and

Bruner 2000; Engel and Munger 2003). Because a key focus of our study was personhood and its transformations, the narrative form provided us with invaluable information and insights.

Certain recurring features in the telling of these stories also illuminate the meaning and significance of the injury narratives. Although we influenced the discursive flow by asking questions that led the narrator in some directions rather than others, our interventions were meant to be delicate, and we could not help observing that some narrative elements recurred whether or not we invited their discussion. There was, in other words, a formulaic quality to the telling of stories about injury. One common element was the multiplicity of causation. Virtually every injury narrative included several causal explanations that appeared on the surface to be mutually exclusive. Typically, the multiple causes of injury included negligence, karma, fate, and the intervention of ghosts or spirits. This recurring narrative pattern led us to the central themes of this book, which we will discuss at length in the chapters that follow.

In addition to the ubiquitous concern with causation, a second element common to the injury narratives is mention of a premonition of harm (*lang sanghon*). Most injury victims make a special point of noting that there had been some sign warning them of danger but they had failed to heed it—the call of an owl, the warnings communicated by a fortune-teller or a neighbor or coworker, or a minor accident that presaged the more serious injury that was about to occur. We think the formulaic reference to an unheeded premonition in each injury narrative serves to underscore the fated nature of the accident and the heavy responsibility that rests on the injury victim him- or herself. If he or she had only been more attentive, if he or she had read the signs more carefully, the harm could have been avoided.

Attention to the discursive conventions of the injury narratives reminds us that telling these stories is itself an act of special significance. The stories are not only windows for viewing things that happened. They can also provide the narrator with a sense of satisfaction that was denied him or her when the actual events unfolded. Simply by telling a story of unfairness, the narrator can transform an unjust occurrence into a performance that discursively enacts justice by assigning or accepting blame or by manifesting forgiveness. For many of our interviewees, achieving justice through narrative was all that was left to them. Telling their stories was not only a way of providing us with "information"; it was also a way of reestablishing order and reaffirming moral values that they believed no longer prevail in contemporary society. By setting things right in their narratives, and by invoking the appropriate terms and concepts, injury victims perform ceremonies of reenactment that may even have karmic significance.

Plan of the Book

The remaining chapters of this book, as we have said, are sandwiched between the personal accounts of Buajan in Chapter 1 and Ming in Chapter 7. Chapter 2 introduces the research site, Chiangmai Province in northern Thailand. We provide a brief history of Chiangmai, giving particular attention to its contacts over many centuries with regional and global influences. We discuss in somewhat greater detail the period of the 1980s and 1990s, when the forces of what was by then called globalization transformed Chiangmai and its people. Chapter 3 discusses two types of legal ordering that have long been a feature of northern Thai society: state law and the law of sacred centers. Throughout the twentieth century, these two forms of legality provided differing ways of mapping injuries onto the physical and social landscape and incorporated different concepts of self, society, authority, and the legal norms that might be applied in injury cases. Despite the differences between state law and the law of sacred centers, however, the interrelationships between them were significant, and the two legal systems in certain ways reinforced and legitimated one another. Chapter 4, however, demonstrates that these interrelationships have been disrupted during the recent era of globalization, which we examine in terms of the twin processes of the relocalization and delocalization of injuries. That is, injuries in contemporary Chiangmai tend to be located far away from the sacred centers that formerly provided an effective system of customary law to resolve such cases; at the same time, the locational significance of harm in general has diminished. The parties now emphasize the despatialized aspects of injuries, which in turn lead injury victims to blame themselves for their mishaps and to abandon potential claims against their injurers.

Chapter 5 shifts the focus to an analysis of injury litigation in the Chiangmai Provincial Court. By comparing litigation patterns in the 1990s to those of the 1960s and 1970s, we are able to suggest that the litigation rates for injury cases appear to have decreased significantly in relation to the probable frequency of injuries in the general population. In this sense, our survey of litigated cases tends to confirm the rejection of law that emerges so strikingly from our interviews with hospitalized injury victims. Content analysis of litigated injury cases further supports the conclusion that state law's connections to traditional customary practices have all but disappeared. In Chapter 6, we ask how these transformations have affected broader perceptions of law and justice among our interviewees. It appears that law and legal institutions are essentially unrelated to our interviewees' concepts of justice. When asked what justice is and how it can be obtained, they never mention law, lawyers, or the courts. The images of justice that they articulate are rooted in religious beliefs and practices that do not correspond to their perceptions of the law. With the loss of customary legal traditions and the rejection of state law, ordinary people in Chiangmai have become deeply pessimistic about the possibility of obtaining justice through existing social institutions. In the wake of the transformations of the late twentieth century, the rule of law seems less attainable—or relevant—than ever before.

1

Buajan's Injury Narrative

A BIRD CHITTERS IN THE TREE at the end of the lane. It is late afternoon, and mosquitoes begin to venture out of the shrubs. Buajan's yard abuts a tall fence with a locked gate. Just beyond the gate we can see the wooded area of a park, formerly the graveyard of a now non-existent temple. Spirits from the graveyard may be listening and could be offended by the things we say, but Buajan must speak honestly with us about her beliefs and experiences: "I wouldn't dare to lie about these things. I'm afraid. I fear sacred things the most."

Buajan was born in a farming village in the neighboring province of Lamphun. She attended primary school in her village and completed the fifth grade before moving to the city of Chiangmai. There she continued her studies through the tenth grade, and there she remained to work as a sales clerk, a cleaner, a launderer, and a cook. She married a native of Chiangmai who is a handyman at a university, and they have two children. Thirty-nine years old at the time of our interview in 1999 and employed on the kitchen staff at a hotel, Buajan struggles to survive Thailand's economic crisis. She earns only 3,000 *baht* per month, which was about $75 at the time of our interview. Buajan describes a recent past filled with setbacks and crises. Of these, the most vivid is the accident that broke her leg and almost took her life.

The Accident

I had just taken my children to school. I drove past Wat Lampoeng, where there's a roadside stand that sells pork. I decided to stop and buy some pork. After I paid for it . . . I was just waiting. . . . This old man, this "Uncle", had . . . parked his car right there, and he began to back up, back, back, back. When he got to the end of the path, he didn't go straight ahead. Instead, he lurched toward me. There was a small child [in a stroller] in his way, and the car was backing into the child, and I went to save him . . . Just then the father pulled the boy away by his arm, but I couldn't get out of the way in time. It was a really big car. I was right here. The car ran into the stroller and went on to smash into a longan tree just behind me and then it bounced off it again. He ran into me. One of my legs was bent and the other was sticking out like this. The car ran right over me and came to a stop, and then it ran over me again.

The roof of the pork stand was collapsing. It was made of corrugated zinc. It would have crushed my neck, but luckily I was wearing a crash helmet so I could push it away. I was conscious. I was able to push it off, but I was really shocked. It was a good thing there was no blood at all, even though my leg was so badly hurt. You can imagine what it was like before the surgery. The driver was shocked, too. If he had seen blood, the guy who hit me, he probably would have died. After they brought me to the hospital, he had to be admitted himself at another hospital. He was an old man, you know? I felt sorry for him. . . .

He said he had no feeling, it was as if someone [Buajan is referring to a ghost] was pushing his car. That's what he told me. At the corner of that shop, there had been fatal accidents. Three or four children had been killed. . . . The pork shop is near a mango tree, which is where I was standing. And near the mango tree, a lot of people had died [indicating the presence of a ghost].

After he hit me he just sat in his car in a state of shock. The villagers took me to the hospital. . . . They put on a splint for support, because the bones were broken, both of them. . . . Later the old man came to see me one time. He came and said something like, "You don't have to report this, right? I'll take care of things. I'll pay all

your expenses." . . . Then he just disappeared. His son came to visit
me when I had my surgery. He came, but he didn't say much. He just
visited and brought me a gift. He came to see me while I was hurting,
and then he disappeared.

Buajan's conversation constantly turns to religious interpretations
of everyday experiences and to her own daily efforts to give expression to
her beliefs. She articulates her spirituality in several different vocabularies.
At times she speaks explicitly of Buddhist-related practices, comment-
ing, for example, that she prays to a Buddha image every day. Buajan's
conversation is also dominated by references to spirits and ghosts. It is
no exaggeration to say that her everyday perceptions and actions revolve
around the spirit world. Whenever she visits her family's home in Lamphun, Buajan propitiates the household spirits and the village guardian
spirits. These ceremonies are obligatory on special occasions, such as her
wedding, the birth of her children, and when members of her family
become ill.

Like many interviewees, she says her beliefs in the supernatural are
"fifty-fifty." She still believes in traditional practices related to the spirits
of northern Thailand, such as healing rituals—although she acknowledges that there have been important new technological developments,
especially in medicine, that can benefit her family. Like her parents' generation, Buajan believes that the ghosts around us may attempt to communicate with us. We cannot see them, but they see us. Contact with
ghosts can cause people, especially children, to become startled or ill.
When this happens, their *khwan*, or spiritual essence, may be injured
or fly out of the body, causing a fever for which the cause cannot be determined (the *khwan* and its rituals are discussed in Chapter 3). In such
cases, it is necessary to make a promise, lighting incense and telling the
ghost that if it is the cause of the child's illness the parents will offer it
chicken or sweets when it allows the child to recover.

Injuries, therefore, may originate in efforts by ghosts to communicate with humans, and one appropriate response is to perform rituals
to propitiate the *khwan*. The most dangerous contacts involve ghosts of
persons who died abnormal or violent deaths. Such ghosts are known as
phi tai hong. Initially, Buajan is reluctant even to discuss them. But then
she, like other interviewees, describes the *sut thon* ceremony performed

at the site of a fatal accident to lead the *winyan*, or soul, of the deceased person away from that place where it might otherwise become a dangerous and malevolent ghost. Buajan describes the purpose of the ritual offerings that are presented at the accident site:

> The *winyan* fell there. It must be invited to leave, to float away so it won't stay there. If it stays, it will attempt to contact other people, and soon other *winyan* will fall there as well. They perform this ceremony; I've seen them do it. They still do it today.

During the *sut thon* ceremony, black, white, and red flags are planted at the spot of the accident along with food and incense to symbolize the progression of the *winyan* from darkness and confused disorder into light and spiritual release:

> The black flag represents the *winyan* of the person who died. The white flag leads him away toward the light. Black means darkness. He cannot go anywhere, especially the person who dies an unnatural death (*tai hong*). He can't enter the house of his relatives. He can't go anywhere. It's dark on all eight sides [an idiom meaning one is completely lost and enclosed in darkness]. This is represented by the color black. Then monks and relatives come and make merit there. After their prayers, the white flag leads him to follow the red flag upwards, so he can be released and float up and escape from the darkness. So he can encounter the light, so he can emerge and be reborn.

The *sut thon* ceremony is still widely performed, and travelers can observe flags beside the road where fatal accidents have taken place. Humans, as Buajan and many others still believe, must attempt to ward off the malevolent ghosts that can cause illness or injury, but human efforts are never enough. People who go out of their houses may encounter ghosts at any time, through no fault of their own. This may have been one of the causes of the accident that injured Buajan herself, but there are also other causes and other explanations.

Causation: Sexual Impropriety

> They said that my injury, the accident when the car hit me, it was because a child, a girl related to me, she went and violated our customs. She acted improperly, and it caused my harm. Probably a

girl, if she went with a boy, that violated the customs of the northern region. She shouldn't have done that. By chance, an ancestor [Buajan refers to a spirit] may have been visiting us then, although we weren't aware of it because we couldn't see him, right? He punished us because the adults, the father and mother, they should have warned the girl not to do this. The spirit medium said it was a relative, I don't know who, who did wrong, and it fell on me. By chance, my stars were weak at that time. . . . The spirit may have come to visit just then and saw this.

Causation: Negligence of "Uncle"

I believe he was negligent. He drove a car even though he had really lost the ability to drive well. He was seventy-four, and they shouldn't let him drive anymore. . . . His eyesight was bad, and he had gout, too. So we blame him. He was in poor health. That's how we look at it. He has a disability; everyone knows he suffers from gout. . . .

He didn't take proper precautions. He knew the car was out of control, so why didn't he brake? Instead, he steered the car in my direction. . . . He accepted all the blame. . . . I was just standing there. There's no reason why he should have hit me, when you think about it. . . .

He said he wasn't well. That's just an easy excuse. He had no feeling in his leg. If this case had actually gone to court, he would have been in big trouble.

Causation: Negligence of Buajan Herself

We have to take precautions. Both sides have to take precautions, both the one who hits us and the one who gets hit. We need to watch out, too.

I think that I was also negligent. I wasn't looking ahead and behind. I didn't turn to my left and my right. I heard the sound of a car coming, "Brrrmmm, brrrmmm!" and I thought it was going down the highway. I never thought it would turn into the area where they were selling things. . . .

When I say that I was negligent, I mean that I didn't watch out. If I had been a little more careful, if I had been out of the way just a little bit more, then I probably wouldn't have been this badly hurt.

Causation: The Ghost in the Mango Tree

Truthfully, I don't like to think about it, but it [the ghost] did play a part. . . . There was another vendor, right? And she placed some food as an offering there for the person to eat, the person who had died. And the owner of the pork stand came and pissed all over it. He said, "Hey, let's add a little fish sauce [salty food flavoring]." Yes, it was that guy.

This is what they told me later. [After he desecrated the offering to the ghost] the owner of the pork stand had been sick a lot. . . . His motorcycle had overturned four or five times, but his stars were still strong, when you think about it. Nothing happened to him. But one young kid, a hill tribe person, his motorcycle hit the tree and he lost a patch of his hair, it stuck right onto the tree. And after my accident, in less than a month, a lot of other people had accidents there, too. But now they're making a new road, and it looks like they're going to cut that tree down and throw it away. That should remove the *winyan*.

Just before he ran into me, there was still hair and blood stuck to the tree. I mean that tree, where the kid had run into it, it was still fresh. That accident just happened a few days before. I didn't know about this until the old man told me. He said, "Oh, that ghost was what did it. He must have wanted to eat the *lap* [minced pork]. When the other woman who sold pork presented the offering, the 'Uncle' at the pork stand went and pissed on it. That's why the ghost never ate it. It must have been a starving ghost." . . .

He blamed the ghost. That was his excuse. He tried to get out of it by saying the ghost did it. Actually, I half believe it, too. Most likely, it really did want something to eat. But I don't live in that village, so there's no way I could have known. If I'd known, I probably would have made something to give it [as an offering].

Causation: *Khro* (Fate)[1]

If we want to consider this in depth, the cause would be the *khro* that we created before that time, and then it came back and caught up with us. We don't know when. We don't know what previous existence it was when we did this. It comes back to us in this existence, at this time. Often we don't know, right? We may have struck a dog or a chicken and broken its leg. Or sometimes we didn't do it, our husband or our children were the ones who did it, but it falls directly on us just because our stars are not especially good at that time.

The accident happened just before my birthday. I was born in April. For a woman, if her age is an odd number, we know it's not very good. She will have *khro*. For men, it's even numbers, and it's especially bad when his age ends in zero. Just by chance, in my case, it was my thirty-ninth birthday when I was injured. . . .

Causation: Karma

Our karma, we don't know when we created it. Maybe we stepped on an ant or something like that, and we consider that karma. We may kill a cockroach without intending it. We may close the bathroom door, and a house lizard that was there might get caught in the door and die. We consider this to be karma that we didn't intend to create.

Once I struck a chicken. It had come up into the house. At that time we were raising chickens. It left its droppings in the house and made a mess. I struck it. And a dog, too. I broke the dog's leg.[2] It was stubborn; I tried to get it to leave the house, but it wouldn't leave. It liked to climb up and lie down near us in the house, on the bed. So I got a stick and hit the dog to drive it out. I think about all of these factors combined. They did play a part.

Comparing the Causes

I think the primary cause was the place, the tree, and also "Uncle." It was Uncle, because he had *khro*. If he had been the one standing there where I was, he probably would have been badly injured. But as it happened, he was protected in the car, which was steel wrapped all around him. That's why he wasn't hurt. But he, in his spirit, he was injured and sick.

Buajan ascribes her accident to numerous causes: a young girl's sexual impropriety that offended an ancestral spirit, the driver's negligence, her own negligence, a hungry ghost near the mango tree, the fact that her age was an odd number of years, and her own karma arising from bad deeds in a previous life or from harm she had inflicted during this life on a dog and chicken. Each causal explanation suggests a different framework for understanding the nature of the injury and how it should be remedied. Assigning responsibility for harm implies an assumption about what should be done next and who should do it. Buajan's narrative mentions several different kinds of remedies, each connected to a different system of social order and normative enforcement: the community of locality-based spirits, the realm of the supernatural, Buddhist beliefs and practices, and governmental institutions.

Remedies: The *Khwan* Ceremony

My mother bound my wrists [with sacred thread, a ritual to secure the *khwan*-soul in the body]. "Uncle" also had a spiritual teacher who went to perform the *sut thon* ceremony, because he was afraid that my *khwan* fell at that spot. He went to retrieve my *khwan* and then bound my wrists with sacred thread. . . . He went to the spot where the accident occurred and scooped up the *khwan*. He did it himself and made a ball of rice, which he placed at the head of my bed. Then he bound my wrists. . . . That helped my mind and spirit.

Remedies: Merit Making

I went to offer food to the monks. I also released some caged birds. I presented the offerings thinking that I might have some bad karma from people I'd wronged in the past. Then I performed the *kruat nam* ceremony [pouring water into a vessel while the monks chant]. I made these offerings for the angels, and for my father and mother who had died, and for my grandparents. Also for anyone I might have wronged or the various wandering souls who might want to eat with us but aren't able to join with us.

Remedies: Negotiating a Settlement

When I got out of the hospital, I had my husband phone "Uncle" to ask him to clear the debt. But "Uncle" said he had already done that when he paid us 20,000 *baht*. Just three or four days after my surgery, he had gone with my husband to notify the police about

PLATE 1.1 *The spirit medium ties sacred string around the wrist of a villager to bind the* khwan *in her body. (David M. Engel)*

the accident. But they didn't actually report it. "Uncle" asked that they settle it privately at the *kamnan's* house [house of the subdistrict officer]. That *kamnan* was probably his relative. So when I got out of the hospital . . . after four or five days, he came to visit. It was just an ordinary visit. I talked to him about my hospital expenses. I made a point of calling him "father" or "grandfather." I said, "Grandfather, we've already spent 15,000 *baht*." At first he said he would "clear" all the costs, but later on he said everything was included in the 20,000 *baht* he had already paid, what he had called payment for the *khwan* (*kha tham khwan*). In the end, he wouldn't agree. I told him, "Uncle, when you talked with me at the hospital, you said you would take care of everything, including my lost wages for each month. But now you're going back on what you told me." He went back on it, and he wouldn't give in.

    We went to the police station. . . . My husband spoke, because I didn't actually go there. The police officer scolded him, saying that

"Uncle" had informed them that he was going to settle with the complainant. So the police officer said, "If you reached a settlement, why are you coming to the police station? A settlement means that there won't be any case or conflict. You reached an agreement outside." . . .

"Uncle" had said we didn't have to worry. As long as I was hurting, he would take care of us. He would pay 2,000 each month, or something like that. And the 20,000 was *"kha tham khwan."* That's what he said. . . .

Later, I went to talk with him. I said I didn't want to make a case out of it, but he had to understand my situation. I had to stop working, and the hotel didn't pay my salary. . . . I said, you should have some sympathy for me. I don't want to sue, but I wasn't the one in the wrong. I could sue for everything. He said, "Oh." I really wasn't asking for much. For my lost wages I asked 15,000 *baht*. That was just for lost wages, but that didn't include the costs for my injured leg. We didn't really finish talking, when he offered me 10,000 *baht*. So I got 30,000 altogether. There was no fine, because I never filed a complaint. If I had, he would have been fined.

Remedies: Signing the Release

At first I thought I might go ahead with this case, but I didn't want any more problems. I'd had enough. Let it end there. That day I went to sign at the lawyer's office. We went to "Uncle's" lawyer. He drew up a document. . . . [Uncle] was afraid that I might sue him later. I signed to show that I had received the money . . . and I wouldn't bring any civil or criminal case.

Buajan sees little connection between law and what she terms justice (*khwam pen tham*). For her, fortune and misfortune arise primarily because of destiny, karma, ghosts, and spirits. The person who seeks justice should not rely on law or lawyers. Buajan's attention to ritual and the propitiation of spirits provides the best guarantee of security for the future and for the redress of past harms. Buajan does not completely ignore the use of law or legal institutions. She does remind "Uncle" that she could pursue a lawsuit if she were so inclined—the *only* spontaneous reference to litigation among all the injury narratives in the entire research project. Yet Buajan regards law and legal institutions with fear. For her, "law" involves powerful and potentially dangerous government officials. When we asked her about law (*kotmai*), she responded that law is slippery and tends to favor the rich and powerful:

> Whenever I've used the law, I've gotten nothing. The police, for example. Law and the police. The law is loose and leaky. That's how it is here. Especially if we're poor, we can't rely on the police for help. Money is more important. That's why I don't rely on the law; I rely on myself.

For Buajan, the legal advantages enjoyed by rich and powerful individuals contrast sharply with the disadvantages of those like herself who are poor but honest: "Today, people who tell the truth, honest people, can't really receive justice. Now people like to lie and cheat."

Buajan concedes that she might have pursued her legal claim against the elderly driver who injured her, but the release she signed prevented her from doing so. It is impossible to know whether she really would have pursued the matter if she had not signed the release. Her general distrust of the legal system and the unreceptiveness of the police to her claim suggest that it is unlikely. Nevertheless, she considers the signing of the release to be another indication of the ways in which rich people can make the law work for them. For ordinary people like herself, justice should not be sought in the law or in legal institutions:

Receiving Justice

> I didn't receive justice. I went to see the duty officer at the police station. He said he wouldn't take the complaint. He wouldn't do anything for me. He advised me to go and arrange a settlement first. I could always file a complaint later. And don't ask for too much. That's what he told me, even though I wasn't the one in the wrong. I felt that I couldn't rely on him. If I tried to bring a case, he might retaliate. I really came out badly, especially because I was a person with no resources. When I thought about it, it wasn't worth it, so I never filed a complaint. Even if I had, he could have turned it all around and made me out to be the one in the wrong.[3]

It's probably because of money. I don't know, I don't know the exact reason. Because these people, the police, they must have been related to "Uncle." His relatives were *kamnan* and police officers and subdistrict councilors. They help each other out. But I don't know anyone. Who would help me?

No matter how holy the law is, I have no hope of using it. I don't stand on the law, I stand on my own two legs, even though one of them is broken.

2

Chiangmai: A History of Globalizations

CHIANGMAI, THAILAND, OFFERS AN IDEAL SETTING in which to trace the connections between global change and new forms of legal consciousness. Chiangmai City (or simply, "Chiangmai"—the names of the province and its capital city are used interchangeably) is the "new city"[1] founded in the late thirteenth century by the legendary leader King Mengrai. Now a bustling metropolis, Chiangmai has long been the economic and cultural center of northern Thailand. Yet a Rip van Winkle who fell asleep in Chiangmai during the mid-1970s would awaken at the turn of the twenty-first century to a city he scarcely recognized. Alarmed by the noise and traffic congestion in the narrow streets, he might wander in confusion among the huge air-conditioned shopping malls, the towering tourist hotels, the cheap guest houses and bustling Night Bazaar, the Internet cafes and coffee houses, the numerous new schools and colleges, the modern government buildings, and the rumble of jumbo jets arriving almost hourly from Bangkok with thousands of tourists and business travelers. Admittedly, he would see some familiar landmarks: the remains of the fortified brick walls and moat surrounding the old city, the base of the massive stupa of Wat Chedi Luang, the ornate artistry of Wat Phra Sing, and the distant golden glitter of Wat Phrathat Doi Suthep on the sacred mountain crest overlooking the city. Yet these landmarks would provide only partial reassurance to the dazed returnee, who would find them dwarfed or obscured by new buildings and roadways and by the noise, chaos, and pollution of a sprawling city that had sprung up in place of the relaxed and picturesque provincial capital he remembers.

Chiangmai's long history of transnational interactions complicates any attempt to study Thai legal consciousness "before and after" globalization. Yet there can be little doubt concerning the extent of the social transformation that Chiangmai experienced during the late twentieth and early twenty-first centuries. Prior to the 1980s, Chiangmai was one of the more cosmopolitan of Thailand's upcountry cities and was exposed to a variety of national and international influences, but such exposures have increased exponentially over the past quarter-century. At the same time, the city, with a population of 171,712 in the year 2000 (the population of the entire province was 1,590,327), has expanded into the outlying countryside, and new superhighways now link Chiangmai to central Thailand, to other northern cities, and soon, perhaps, across Laos to nearby China. Developers have bought up farmland and converted it to condominiums and shopping centers. Internal migrations have brought villagers and residents of other Thai regions to the city of Chiangmai. Particularly in urban areas, the distinctive northern Thai dialect is increasingly displaced by central dialect as the language of everyday speech.

Chiangmai, like the rest of Thailand, experienced a series of economic highs and lows during the past few decades. The boom years of the 1980s and early 1990s were followed by the financial crisis of 1997, which in turn gave way to a period of steady recovery in the first decade of the twenty-first century. Despite these dramatic swings, the general pattern over the past quarter-century has been one of growth and expansion. Village society has been depopulated, as we can see in the accounts of interviewees such as Buajan. Disparities in the distribution of wealth and social power have become more pronounced. New systems of communication, which Giddens (2003, 10) cites as particularly important to the process of globalization, have profoundly challenged preexisting worldviews and social practices. Television, film, DVDs, and the Internet have imported new images and ideas from Bangkok and from non-Thai centers of cultural production.

In this chapter, we provide a brief overview of Chiangmai past and present, with a particular emphasis on its history of exposure to global influences from its earliest origins to the contemporary period.

Global Contacts before the Contemporary Era

Chiangmai's geography helps to explain its recurring exposure to regional and transnational forces. The mountainous northern region of Thailand, covered by dense green forests, is in fact the foothills of the Himalayas. Four major rivers—the Ping, the Wang, the Yom, and the Nan—flow south through this region, carving long valleys in the rugged northern landscape. These river valleys were gradually settled by wet-rice cultivators and, as historian David Wyatt suggests, a distinctive Tai[2] civilization probably existed as long as 2,000 years ago (Wyatt 1984, 3–4; see also Baker and Phongpaichit 2005, 3). By the eighth century A.D., according to Wyatt, we may suppose that "the Tai world already was extended across much of northern Southeast Asia." (11).

Yet the Tai peoples never existed in isolation. Their political, economic, cultural, and religious practices were profoundly influenced by exposure to the Dvaravati civilization of the Mon people, the mighty Angkorian empire to the southeast, and the Nan-chao and Chinese empires to the north. Indeed, Chiangmai was founded in the late thirteenth century only as Mongol Chinese power receded from what is now northern Thailand (Wyatt, 43–50). At that time, King Mengrai built his new capital on the banks of the Ping River and constructed the distinctive square-shaped city walls whose remains still define the boundaries of the old city. Under Mengrai's rule, Chiangmai became one of the most important of the Tai principalities and the center of the flourishing Lanna region (*Lanna* means, literally, "a million rice fields").

King Mengrai's descendants governed Chiangmai into the sixteenth century, even as its Siamese neighbors to the south—particularly the increasingly powerful kingdom of Ayutthaya—contended with the Burmese to the west for influence and control. Much of Chiangmai's history reflects the alternations of Siamese and Burmese cultural, political, and military hegemony and the efforts of Chiangmai's rulers to

PLATE 2.1 *Remains of the brick walls surrounding the old city of Chiangmai. (David M. Engel)*

thwart these ambitious neighbors and retain some measure of autonomy. Ultimately, however, Chiangmai's efforts failed, and its destiny was shaped by the more powerful external forces sweeping across the region. In 1558, the Burmese army conquered Chiangmai, subjecting it to two centuries of Burmese rule, first as "a free province of a 'foreign country'" and later as "an integral part of the Burmese kingdom" (Ongsakul 2005, 122). Throughout this period, the Burmese overlords faced challenges from Ayutthaya as well as resistance from Lanna leaders, and localized rebellions and warfare intensified during the eighteenth century. When the Burmese sacked and destroyed Ayutthaya in 1767, they also subdued Lanna, destroying or capturing its people and treasure (Baker and Phongpaichit, 23). Later in the same year, King Taksin, a Siamese leader who had escaped the devastation of Ayutthaya, established a new capital in Thonburi, and Lanna leaders promptly forged an alliance with him in opposition to Burma. With Taksin's assistance, Prince Kawila seized Chiangmai from the Burmese in 1774, but the Burmese soon returned to lay siege to the city. When the siege was broken in 1776, the hungry and impoverished inhabitants of Chiangmai completely abandoned their city (Ongsakul, 131).

In 1782, the short-lived Thonburi dynasty of Taksin was overthrown and replaced by the current Chakri dynasty, founded by King Rama I in Bangkok; and "King" Kawila[3] reestablished control of Chiangmai despite continued Burmese hegemony elsewhere in Lanna. A period of repopulation ensued from 1782 to 1813, known as "putting vegetables into baskets and people into towns" (Kraisri Nimmanhaeminda 1965; Ongsakul, 132). By attacking and capturing the populations of towns throughout the north and relocating them in Chiangmai, Kawila solved Chiangmai's labor crisis and at the same time produced a demographic crazy quilt in the principality's resettled towns and villages. The history of regional battles and struggles for local autonomy in the eighteenth and early nineteenth centuries therefore explains the extraordinary ethnic and cultural heterogeneity of rural Chiangmai today, where the inhabitants of neighboring villages may trace their roots to—and derive their cultural practices from—diverse and distant ancestral homes.[4]

The nineteenth and early twentieth centuries brought other forms of contact with regional and global powers with equally significant

consequences for Chiangmai's future. Chiangmai settled into a tributary relationship with the emergent Chakri dynasty, but local autonomy
was increasingly threatened by competition between the Siamese and the
British imperialists, who were gaining control of Burma to Chiangmai's
west. During the reign of King Rama V (1868–1910), disputes with the
British over legal matters, including teak concessions and the safety of
British subjects in Lanna, led to treaties in 1874 and 1883 providing for
binational adjudication in special courts.[5] Rama V took this opportunity
to curb the power of local princes and subject Lanna more extensively
to central Siamese control. He recognized that, by drafting European-
style law codes and devising a national court system administered from
Bangkok, he could respond to complaints by European governments
that their citizens and commercial dealings were inadequately protected.
Thus, legal modernization became a tool of national integration and
survival in the face of imperialist threats. The urgency of this task was
underscored by conflicts with France over territorial claims along what
is now Thailand's boundary with Laos and with the British over what is
now the Thai–Malay boundary in the southern peninsula. Rama V concluded that he could preserve his country's independence and territorial
integrity only by consolidating central control, creating a European-style
legal system, and presenting Siam to the world as a "modern" nation-
state (see generally Winichakul 1994; Wyatt 1984, 202–208; Baker and
Phongpaichit 2005, 58–61).

Drawing on the talents of Thai and foreign legal experts, Rama
V launched a transformation of the Thai legal system under the leader-
ship of his son, Prince Ratburi Direkrit, widely known as the "father
of Thai law." The work of legal reform proceeded apace (see Engel 1975
and 1978; Loos 2006; Harding 2008). In 1896, the Law of the Provincial
Courts created a three-level judiciary in the regions outside Bangkok, including Chiangmai. In 1908, the Law of the Courts of Justice transferred
control of the provincial court system from the Ministry of Interior to
the Ministry of Justice, headed by Prince Ratburi. A law of evidence was
promulgated in 1895, provisional codes of criminal and civil procedure
in 1896, and the Penal Code in 1908. The codification process continued
after the death of Rama V in 1910. Between 1924 and 1935, the six books

of the Civil and Commercial Code were enacted, and permanent codes of criminal and civil procedure appeared in 1935.

At the same time that he initiated his legal reforms, Rama V attempted to extricate Chiangmai and the north from the potential grasp of the British by incorporating them more securely into the Siamese polity. He achieved this, with Minister of the Interior Prince Damrong Rajanupab (his half-brother), by establishing a nationwide *thesaphiban* administrative system, consisting of twenty regions (*monthon*), each headed by a royal commissioner (Vickery 1970, 876; Ramsay 1971, 260–266; Bunnag 1977). As a result, Chiangmai was transformed from a semiautonomous tributary state to a unit within the *thesaphiban* structure of the Siamese nation. As the capital of the northern Phayap region, Chiangmai was initially allowed to retain some of its traditional practices and rulers, but real power was now vested in the officials of the Siamese central government and the judiciary. It was not long before civil servants replaced local leaders and Chiangmai's distinctive laws and practices were entirely supplanted by those of the national government in Bangkok. By the time the *thesaphiban* system was abolished in 1933, Chiangmai had become no different from any other province in status and political identity. The locus of political authority had shifted southward to Bangkok. Chiangmai residents could only observe from a distance when important political developments took place in the nation's capital, as the absolute monarchy was replaced with a constitutional system in 1932 and as military rule alternated with democracy throughout the remainder of the twentieth century.

Today, despite its size and importance as a regional center, Chiangmai is but one of seventy-five provinces in the modern state of Thailand, as the country became known in 1939. Like the rest of Thailand, Chiangmai continued to experience global contacts and influences throughout the modern era. During World War II, the Japanese occupied Thailand, although a Free Thai resistance movement allied itself with the English and American forces. After the war, Thailand became the subject of intense American efforts to combat Asian communism. Thailand sent soldiers to fight in the Korean War, joined SEATO (South-East Asian Treaty Organization), and assisted the United States in the Vietnam War effort by sending military personnel and by permitting the Americans to construct enormous airbases to launch bombing runs over Vietnam, Cambodia, and Laos. Not coincidentally, Thailand's "American era" (Baker and Phongpaichit 2005, 140) was also characterized by a series of military dictatorships and coups d'état.

In the 1960s, Chiangmai became a center for American and other international personnel attempting to suppress the drug trade and the antigovernment guerilla movement. During this same period, global tourism and international investment activity became more evident in Chiangmai, as they did throughout Thailand, and commercial relations with Japan, Europe, the United States, and China expanded steadily. In the run-up to the period now labeled the era of globalization, all of these global contacts quickened and were reflected as well in Chiangmai's popular culture and media—music, film, fashion, radio, and television—with influences from sources as diverse as India, China, the United States, Japan, Europe, and the United Kingdom.

Globalization in Chiangmai from 1975 to the Present

Global forces in the late twentieth and early twenty-first centuries have shaped Chiangmai in new and different ways. The period from 1975 to the present is of particular interest in this book. In 1975, we had our first opportunity to conduct research on injuries, litigation, and legal consciousness in Chiangmai (see Engel 1978). Since then, Chiangmai has grown and changed substantially. In the chapters that follow, we ask what changes in the legal practices and legal consciousness of ordinary people have accompanied these social transformations.

What, then, is meant by the term *globalization* as applied to the current era, and how do the transformations of the late twentieth and early twenty-first centuries differ—if at all—from earlier periods of global interaction and social change? Although it is common to speak of globalization with reference to transnational markets and economic actors, many theorists agree that its effects cannot be measured solely in terms of business relations, multinational corporate activities, or economic development. In Robertson's much-quoted definition (1992, 8), globalization "refers both to the compression of the world and the intensification of consciousness of the world as a whole." Giddens (2003, 10) contends that it is a "mistake" to view globalization only in economic terms: "Globalization is political, technological and cultural, as well as economic. It has been influenced above all by developments in systems of communication, dating back only to the late 1960s." Globalization, in this view, is not just a change in material conditions and relationships but also in the way people think, understand, communicate, and behave. It involves temporal and spatial transformations, a speeding up of contacts and influences, and an interconnecting of hitherto distant locations and peoples:

> First of all, given the development of worldwide modes of transport and communication, globalization implies a speeding up of the flows of capital, people, goods, images, and ideas across the world, thus pointing to a general increase in the pace of global interactions and processes. Second, it suggests an intensification of the links, modes of interaction, and flows that interconnect the world . . . Third, globalization entails a stretching of social, cultural, political, and economic practices across frontiers so as to make possible action at a distance—that is, so that happenings, decisions, and practices in one area of the globe can come to have consequences for communities and cultures in remote locales of the globe. And finally, as a result of all this speeding up, intensification, and stretching, globalization also implies a heightened entanglement of the global and local such that, while everyone might continue to live local lives, their phenomenal worlds have to some extent become global as distant events come to have an impact on local spaces, and local developments come to have global repercussions. (Inda and Rosaldo 2002, 9)

Appadurai (1996, 33–35) suggests that the "global cultural flows" that constitute globalization can be examined through five different dimensions, which he calls ethnoscapes, mediascapes, technoscapes, financescapes, and ideoscapes. Each of these dimensions has relevance to the changes that have taken place over the past quarter-century in Thailand generally and in Chiangmai in particular. We will consider each in turn.

Ethnoscapes are "the landscape of persons who constitute the shifting world in which we live: tourists, immigrants, refugees, exiles, guest workers, and other moving groups and individuals . . ." (Appadurai, 33). Major changes along this dimension are vividly apparent in Chiangmai. Internal migration has been substantial, and the city of Chiangmai in particular has welcomed newcomers from elsewhere in the northern region and from other parts of Thailand. Tourists from Europe, Japan, Australia, North America, China, and the Middle East have flooded Chiangmai province, ranging from wealthy visitors who stay in expensive and luxurious resorts to backpackers who frequent the sometimes seedy guesthouses and bars; from students, scholars, and admirers of the natural environment to druggies and sex tourists. Refugees and undocumented workers from neighboring Myanmar (formerly Burma) constitute a growing segment of the low-wage workforce. Villagers in Chiangmai province have deserted their ancestral homes in search of wage labor in the cities, transforming the demography of rural as well as urban Chiangmai. At the same time, developers have bought up farmland and built condominiums, factories, industrial estates, and shopping centers. As we shall suggest in later chapters, the movement of people from their village communities has great significance for customary and formal legal practices.

Mediascapes refers "both to the distribution of the electronic capabilities to produce and disseminate information (newspapers, magazines, television stations, and film-production studies) . . . and to the images of the world created by these media" (Appadurai, 35). In Chiangmai, televisions are now ubiquitous, and their soap operas, movies, and news broadcasts are favored forms of entertainment. Films from Thailand and around the world are wildly popular in theaters and on DVD. Newspapers and magazines printed in Bangkok are widely read, and they reflect transnational information production as well as domestic interests and concerns. Radio remains a primary medium of entertainment and information distribution. Although local media are popular, Chiangmai residents are increasingly exposed to content produced far from northern Thailand—in Bangkok or in other countries and world regions. They have become part of a global audience that avidly follows sports, entertainment, and politics worldwide.

Appadurai defines *technoscapes* as "the global configuration, also ever fluid, of technology and the fact that technology, both high and low, both mechanical and informational, now moves at high speeds across various kinds of previously impervious boundaries" (34). Chiangmai cannot match Bangkok's astonishing technological advances during the last quarter-century but nonetheless has witnessed changes associated with the arrival of new forms of production and communication. Motorized tillers have replaced water buffalo in the rice fields—and have also been adapted to transport goods and people throughout the rural countryside. Huge highway construction machinery has replaced elephant and human labor. Trucks, cars, and motorcycles have replaced oxcarts on the roadways. Retail stores in the city sell the latest electronic and household devices to an eager throng of consumers. The Internet has linked ordinary citizens, particularly the younger generation, to a world of information, images, trends, and communication opportunities. Mobile phones and text messaging have been adopted with startling proficiency by local residents.

Financescapes refers to "the disposition of global capital . . . as currency markets, national stock exchanges, and commodity speculations move megamonies through national turnstiles at blinding speed" (Appadurai, 34–35). The last quarter of the twentieth century witnessed substantial changes in Thailand's connection to global capital and finance. In the late 1970s, Thai policy makers planned a shift to an export-oriented economy based on increased industrial development. The policy succeeded dramatically in achieving its goals. With the devaluation of the *baht* in relation to the dollar and the yen in 1985, Thai exports grew rapidly. In 1985, manufactured exports totaled $2,800 million, but by 1994 they had risen to $36,618 million (Dixon 1999, 114). Foreign direct investment in Thailand by Japan, the United States, and other countries in Asia and elsewhere rose to a peak of $2.46 billion in 1990 (Phongpaichit and Baker 1998, 39),[6] and joint ventures proliferated. New foreign investment was primarily in industry (see Dixon 1999, 132; Hussey 1993, 17), most of which was located in the Bangkok area. Indeed, in 1999 the six provinces in the Bangkok region,[7] with their heavy concentration of industry, had only 15 percent of Thailand's population yet produced 86 percent of the nation's GDP. By contrast, Chiangmai's northern region had 19 percent of the population but produced only 9 percent of the GDP (UNDP [United Nations Development Programme] 2003, 126–127).

Although Chiangmai has not experienced the dramatic industrial growth that has occurred in the Bangkok area, its economy and society have been radically affected by changes emanating from the Thai capital. Construction has boomed in response to demands of the growing middle class as well as international visitors. Previously unheard-of traffic jams clog the narrow city streets throughout the day, and the city has spilled outward into the countryside.

Thailand's boom years of the 1980s and early 1990s came to a halt with the financial crisis of 1997. A rapid depreciation of the *baht* "was accompanied by the virtual collapse of the property and stock markets" (Dixon 1999, 239). The International Monetary Fund, a leading promoter of globalization, agreed to help bail Thailand out of its crisis but demanded draconian spending cuts and other fiscal reforms. The media soon began to run stories about the "formerly rich," who were selling off their houses and cars and, in some cases, were reduced to street peddlers. For many Thais who had been drawn to Bangkok and other urban centers during the boom years, the crash of 1997 meant a return to the villages—if they were fortunate enough not to have lost their rural homes in the rush to sell land to developers and industrialists—but less than a decade later, a recovery was underway, and the economy resumed its dynamic growth. Needless to say, all of these economic swings had their effects in Chiangmai, as they did throughout Thailand.

Appadurai describes *ideoscapes* as "concatenations of images . . . [that] are often directly political and frequently have to do with the ideologies of states and the counterideologies of movements explicitly oriented to capturing state power or a piece of it" (36). Because of our particular interest in issues of legal consciousness and attitudes toward legal and political institutions, "ideoscapes" are of special relevance to this study. Appadurai suggests that they "are composed of elements of the Enlightenment worldview, which consists of a chain of ideas, terms, and images, including *freedom, welfare, rights, sovereignty, representation*, and the master term *democracy*" (36). Yet the dispersion of such concepts throughout the world "has loosened the internal coherence that held them together in a Euro-American master narrative and provided instead a loosely structured synopticon of politics" (36). Appadurai's reference to a reconfigured version of Euro-American legal and political discourse provides at least a starting point for understanding legal consciousness in contemporary Chiangmai.

Globalized ideologies and practices associated with international rights movements, constitutionalism, and democracy have clearly made their appearance in Chiangmai, yet local actors have expressed these ideologies in a vocabulary that draws on Buddhism and village-level traditions as much as liberal legalism. For example, when developers announced plans to construct an electric cable car that would have disfigured the sacred mountain crest of Doi Suthep overlooking the city of Chiangmai, opponents defeated their efforts by forming an unusual alliance of NGOs, Buddhist clergy, academics, and villagers (Swearer et al. 2004, 33–35). When the government proposed to expand the Chiangmai–Lamphun highway by cutting down the stately rows of rubber trees lining the route, a similar alliance was formed. The trees were ultimately preserved when opponents of the government plan performed a Buddhist ordination ceremony and wrapped all of the trees in saffron-colored cloths, thereby saving them from destruction. Both examples suggest that rights movements in Chiangmai are not simple expressions of Euro-American legal ideologies but should be understood in terms of a legal consciousness in which Buddhism and other village-based belief systems play a central role. As the later chapters of this book suggest, this form of legal-religious consciousness rather than more familiar forms of liberal legalism emerges with considerable clarity in the injury narratives of our interviewees.

Conclusion

From this brief overview of global contacts and interactions throughout Chiangmai's history, it should be apparent that the city and province have long been exposed to the influence of other peoples and nations. The impact of global forces had particular significance during the reign of King Rama V, when the threat of the great colonial powers—England and France—on the borders led to the transformation of the nation's political and legal systems and the incorporation of Chiangmai into the modern nation-state. This earlier encounter with powerful global forces transformed the Thai polity and served as an important precursor to Thailand's more recent experience with globalization in the late twentieth century.

Although it would be incorrect to say that Thailand's exposure to global influences in the last quarter of the twentieth century was unprecedented in its history, it cannot be denied that radical changes have taken place in Chiangmai, just as they have in Thailand as a whole. Across all the dimensions identified by Appadurai—ethnoscapes, mediascapes, technoscapes, financescapes, and ideoscapes—Chiangmai has changed in very significant ways, and its residents' lives and consciousness have been transformed. The world has indeed been compressed. Awareness of the world and each individual's place in it are no longer what they were prior to 1975. The lives of ordinary people have changed as many of them pursue their everyday activities in new settings and undertake new tasks in the context of new social and economic relationships. Family structures and living arrangements have changed. Transportation and communication have been transformed. Connections to village society have become attenuated. Religious practices have been altered. In the chapters that follow, we will explore the implications of these changes for law and legal consciousness.

3

State Law and the Law of Sacred Centers

HAVING OUTLINED THE GLOBAL INFLUENCES to which Chiangmai was exposed in the late twentieth century, we now examine their interaction with legal consciousness. We focus in particular on injuries and the ways ordinary people interpret and respond to them. Our insights are drawn primarily from interviews with seriously injured men and women and with other individuals who helped to shed light on both customary and official legal practices in Chiangmai. We interpret these interview materials with particular attention to the five key elements of culture and consciousness discussed in the Introduction: (1) spatial and temporal frameworks; (2) concepts of the self; (3) community, social networks, and relationships; (4) justice norms and procedures; and (5) cosmology and religious belief.

In this chapter, we compare two fundamentally different concepts of law that emerged clearly from our interviews, state law and the nonstate law of sacred centers. These two conceptualizations of law reflect distinctive spatial and temporal frameworks that lead people to differing views of self and community and of justice itself. Our discussion of state law will be relatively brief because this conception of legality is so familiar in the modern era as to be axiomatic. We will discuss the law of sacred centers at greater length because it involves beliefs and practices

that were well known to the parents and grandparents of our interviewees but are somewhat less familiar to contemporary Thais and not at
all familiar to most non-Thais. To consider the law of sacred centers,
therefore, we must delve back into the past, into a world remembered by
our interviewees with varying degrees of clarity.

Although our discussion of the law of sacred centers will return
us to an earlier era, the interviewees' journeys back in time were also
journeys across space, from the locations where they live as adults to
the locations where they grew up. The move to new, often urban, settings was associated in their minds with the loss of the older generation's
traditional beliefs and practices. Moreover, in many cases their parents
and older relatives still lived in those childhood locations. When individuals suffered injuries, the elders frequently intervened and invoked
traditional practices that had sometimes grown dim in the understandings of the injured persons themselves. The narratives we recorded are
suffused by a nostalgic longing for customs the interviewees now feel
unable to observe. Although some individuals viewed the old ways with
disdain, others worried that important traditions would be lost when the
older generation died off, and injury victims would be cast adrift in a
new world where interpretations of cause, effect, and responsibility were
confused and the obligation to provide compensation was uncertain.

In this chapter, then, we distinguish the two conceptions of law
that held the most significance for our interviewees and explore in some
detail the beliefs and practices associated with an older generation and
with the village communities left behind by most of the injury victims.
We examine the interactions and interconnections between these two
forms of legality. In the next chapter, we will ask how these interactions
and interconnections have changed with the effects of globalization.

State Law and Injuries in Thailand

When King Rama III displayed a Siamese map to a group of Eu-
ropeans who visited his court in the 1840s, they could scarcely contain
their laughter.[1] According to one English eyewitness, the map depicted
the kingdom of Siam and its bothersome neighbor, Burma, but it did
not observe the conventions of European cartography. Rather, accord-

ing to the English visitor, the "map" consisted of a silvery cartoonlike figure representing the Siamese king drawn on a large red rectangular field surrounded by pictures of boats floating in the water. Above the red field representing Siam was a less imposing green rectangular field with a small and unflattering black cartoon of the king of Burma surrounded by his subjects, who were depicted as tiny dancing imps. Between the red and green fields, the mapmaker had drawn the boundary as a black horizontal stripe with a squiggly line on the Siamese side designating territory falsely claimed by the Burmese monarch. This graphic representation conceived of the two kingdoms, which actually lie to the east and west of one another and not to the north and south, in terms of the rulers themselves and national territory as emanating outward from their bodies. The map depicted the greater and more virtuous space surrounding the Siamese king as a "celestial domain" and the lesser space surrounding the Burmese king as the "domain of demons" (Winichakul 1994, 35).

During the next half-century, successors to the Siamese throne would draw quite different maps of their country. Relying on Western surveyors and European concepts of cartography, King Rama V in the late nineteenth century established the boundary lines of a kingdom within which he could claim rights of sovereignty and fend off the English and French, who occupied neighboring countries (Winichakul, 121; see also Engel 1975 and 1978). Inside this national perimeter, he promulgated the *thesaphiban* system, consisting of *monthon*, or administrative circles, which in turn contained nested subunits—provinces, districts, subdistricts, and villages (Engel 1978; Winichakul). The *thesaphiban* system supplanted an administrative model that Tambiah (1976, 102–131) has termed a "galactic" polity, configured according to Hindu-Buddhist "cosmological topography," in which the royal capital "was surrounded by a circle of provinces ruled by princes or governors appointed by the king, and these again were surrounded by more or less independent 'tributary' polities" (Id., 112). Rama V replaced the older imagining of geopolitical space with a grid, which located all political centers and rulers within the redefined space of the nation and eventually subjected them to laws and regulations formulated in Bangkok.[2]

This process of political and spatial transformation in the creation of the modern nation-state was not unique to Thailand. Anderson (1991,

19) identifies a similar set of developments throughout Southeast Asia and elsewhere and describes how "dynastic realms" gave way to nation-states. In the traditional dynastic realm, according to Anderson, "kingship organizes everything around a high centre" legitimated by sacred connections and authority. But sacred centers have no significance in the demarcation of political authority in the modern nation-state, where "sovereignty is fully, flatly, and evenly operative over each square centimeter of a legally demarcated territory."

The "modern" state develops new ways of seeing and new technologies of measuring and mapping (Scott 1998). Cadastral surveys fix the boundaries of smaller landholdings as well as larger political units. Household properties, villages, towns, and provincial capitals are defined by their perimeters rather than by sacred centers marked with pillars or shrines. Within these boundaries, humans acquire new identities as citizens who are situated in particular geopolitical administrative units, counted by national surveys, taxed by the central government, conscripted by the military draft, and subjected to a set of universally applicable legal rights and obligations.[3]

The latter type of legal map is the sine qua non of state law. It is so familiar that it requires some effort to recognize the distinctive spatial and temporal framework on which state law depends. Every schoolchild learns the map of his or her country and the concept that the state's legal and political authority extends pervasively and (in theory) uniformly within national borders. Lawyers implicitly rely on this form of legal mapping when they refer to law's jurisdiction as coterminous with geographic boundaries, regardless of the diverse communities and cultures such boundaries might enclose. Sociolegal theorists, from Weber to the present, also tend to regard the state's mapping of law as an essential act of creation:

> In the past, Weber said, law arose as "volitive" and as "particularistic" law, based on the agreed enactment of consensual status groups. There were different legal communities, constituted in their membership by personal characteristics such as birth, political, ethnic or religious denomination, mode of life or occupation, and so on. Individuals or groups of individuals had their own personal legal quality, and carried their law,

PLATE 3.1 *Structure at Wat Chedi Luang, Chiangmai, housing the pillar* (lak mǔang) *marking the sacred center of Chiangmai. (Patrick Whitaker)*

their *profession juris*, with them wherever they went. . . . The idea of a law of the land developed only very gradually—the *lex terrae*, which was applicable to everyone regardless of personal characteristics, and imposed as a heteronomous law within the boundaries of a given territory.[4]

Contemporary sociolegal scholars have sought in particular to explain how modern governments create maps of the entirety of their terrain and then measure, simplify, standardize, and assert power over the peoples and social practices within (Foucault 1980, 68–69: Harvey 1990, 249–50; Scott 1998). Yet, the state's effort to enclose a territory and impose legal order on it can never supplant all other legal orderings and other mappings. Modern law never fully occupies the space over which it claims sovereignty (e.g., Galanter 1974; de Certeau 1984; Santos 1995; Fitzpatrick 2005) but must inevitably interact with other unofficial or quasi-official legal orders in society. Weber in his classic study, *Economy and Society* (1978, 316–317), wrote, "[W]e categorically deny that 'law' exists only where legal coercion is guaranteed by the political authority" and insisted that state law must be understood in terms of its mutually dependent relationship with nonstate legal systems. Contemporary law and society scholars have often expressed agreement with this perspective. Galanter (1974, 126–127), for example, describes the function of state law and its role in everyday life in terms of its connections to dispute settlement systems "appended to the official system" and other "informal systems of 'private justice' which invoke other norms and other sanctions." Santos (1995) employs the metaphor of the map to describe what he calls the "interplay" between different forms and scales of legal regulation. Fitzpatrick (2005, 9) describes the paradox of modern law, which "must assert a fixed and determinate position within its sphere, yet it must remain 'infinitely responsive' to that which is outside legal norms (i.e. culture and society)."

Yet the inevitable interconnections between state law and nonofficial legal orders are not necessarily acknowledged by state actors or by the legal systems they enforce. Indeed, it is often the purpose of state law to root out nonstate law and to assert exclusive control over the legal practices of all citizens. This was certainly the case in Thailand, where the monarchy aimed to eliminate rival centers of regional political and legal authority and to impose a uniform system of law controlled from the capital. As we have seen, Thailand's substantive and procedural law codes were in place by 1935. The current court system emerged at about the same time with the enactment of the Charter of the Courts of Justice (*phra thammanun san yuttitham*), first promulgated in 1935 and amended periodically thereafter. According to the Charter, each province has both a Provincial Court of general jurisdiction and a Magistrates' Court for minor criminal and civil matters. Appeals from courts of first instance go to the Court of Appeals in Bangkok and thence to the Supreme (*dika*) Court.[5]

The laws pertaining to injury cases·that were litigated in the state court system made no acknowledgment of customary practices. Individuals who suffered injuries could invoke Thai tort law or, in some instances, could mobilize Thai criminal law as a private prosecutor. The general framework of Thai tort law is addressed by Title V, "Wrongful Acts," of the Thai Civil and Commercial Code, although specific types of torts can also be created by statute.[6] Title V is divided into three chapters: "Liability for Wrongful Acts" (§§420–437), "Compensation for Wrongful Acts" (§§438–448), and "Defenses" (§§449–552). The foundational statement concerning the Thai law of wrongful acts appears in the initial provision of Title V:

> Section 420. A person who, willfully or negligently, unlawfully injures the life, body, health, liberty, property, or any right of another person, is said to commit a wrongful act and is bound to make compensation therefor.

"Willfully" means acting with an awareness that one's actions will cause harm to another, even if the actor does not desire to inflict a particular injury (Supphanit 1994, 16). "Negligence" is not defined in the Civil and Commercial Code, but comparison to the definition contained in the Thai Penal Code[7] leads one author (Id. 18) to define negligence in the tort context as follows: "Acting in a non-willful manner but without the degree of care that a person in such a situation must exercise considering his or her capabilities and the existing circumstances." The term *unlawfully* in Section 420 refers not only to violations of particular laws or statutes but more generally to negligent acts resulting in injuries that the actor had no authority or right to inflict on another (Id. 23; Wannasaeng 1995, 17).

The compensation provisions of Title V, insofar as they address torts causing personal injury, require the tortfeasor to reimburse the victim's "expenses and damages for total or partial disability to work, for the present as well as for the future" (Section 444) and also to provide "compensation for damage which is not a pecuniary loss" (Section 446). If the tortfeasor's actions result in death, he or she must pay "funeral and other necessary expenses" (Section 443). If death does not occur immediately, the tortfeasor is also liable for lost wages, medical treatment, and damages that accrue prior to death (Id.). In both injury and wrongful death cases, the tortfeasor must also compensate any third parties who have suffered losses because of the inability of the injured person to perform services that he or she was bound by law to perform in the household or in a work setting.

In addition to bringing a civil suit for damages, an injured person has another option under Thai law—a private criminal action. The Thai Criminal Procedure Code provides that a criminal prosecution may be brought *either* by the public prosecutor or by "the injured person" (Section 28). Even when the public prosecutor has already initiated a criminal prosecution, the injured person may elect to join as prosecutor "at any stage of the proceedings before the pronouncement of judgment by the court of first instance" (Section 30). In private criminal actions, the defendant's conduct is evaluated according to the provisions of the Penal Code rather than Thai tort law. Furthermore, the ostensible purpose of bringing a private criminal action is to impose punishment rather than to obtain compensation. Nevertheless, injury victims in Thailand sometimes bring private criminal actions to gain leverage in their extrajudicial negotiations with the defendant. If the defendant pays compensation, the injured party may agree to withdraw the prosecution, even though such agreements tend to violate the spirit and the letter of the criminal law (Petchsiri 1987, 175). Functionally, therefore, the private criminal prosecution serves a purpose similar to a tort action.

From this brief summary, we may conclude that injury victims in Chiangmai can pursue a remedy in the state law system by bringing either a tort or private criminal action in the provincial court. State law has unique features that distinguish it from the nonstate legal systems that may be available to injured persons:

1. State law operates within precisely delimited spatial boundaries. The power of the court is effective throughout its carefully mapped geographical jurisdiction and is not more intense in some spatial locations than others (unlike the law of sacred centers, as we shall see).

2. State law also operates within precisely delimited temporal boundaries. In injury cases, state law considers only the temporally compact cluster of events immediately associated with the injury, as opposed to aspects of the dispute relationship that may have transpired years before the injury or even in a prior lifetime. Furthermore, the operation of state law is temporally bounded by the time limitations imposed on plaintiffs for litigating their claims.

3. State law professes to operate without explicit regard for the particular community or cultural or ethnic group of the parties. Although such groups might have distinctive norms or practices concerning injuries and might characterize the parties in distinctive ways, state law deliberately "blinds" itself to such distinctions (as symbolized by the figure of justice wearing a blindfold) and purports to treat all parties the same.

4. State law is preserved in written form and must be published and disseminated before the genesis of the cases to which it is applied. Its norms are formulated to be neutral, abstract, and general in application. They derive from Anglo-European jurisprudence and in injury cases have no overt connection to Thai religious or philosophical traditions.

5. Judges in the state law system should be strangers to the parties and their social networks, unlike trusted elders in nonstate systems who have firsthand knowledge of the dispute and the disputants. Judges' authority derives from the state that employs them and the king whom they symbolically represent, not from their association with local groups, social networks, or supernatural elements.

6. The parties are individual citizens of the state, not families, kin groups, or village communities. In state law, the parties appear before the court disconnected from their social networks, even if their own self-concept is collective rather than the radically individualized identity imposed on them by the official legal system.

These, then, are some of the most distinctive features of state law, particularly as it operates in Thai injury cases. As we shall see in the next section, these features stand in sharp contrast to those of nonstate law, in particular the customary system we call the law of sacred centers. The two systems rest on radically different concepts of space, time, identity, norms, procedures, and theories of justice. Although state law would in theory deny the legitimacy and even the existence of the law of sacred centers, the two systems were, as sociolegal theorists have long observed, interconnected. We now turn to a description of the law of sacred centers and its relationship to state law.

Law of Sacred Centers in the Village

We have said that the law of sacred centers radiates outward from a locus having supernatural potency. This system of unwritten customary norms and procedures is strongest at locations closest to the center and becomes weaker and more uncertain at more distant locations. People in Chiangmai remember the law of sacred centers as a feature of village life during their childhood, and they associate it with the traditional practices of their parents and grandparents. We begin our description, therefore, with our interviewees' recollections of the villages and households into which they were born.

The household was historically the sacred center that shaped the identity of Thai villagers from the beginning of their lives. In the past, according to the recollections of many interviewees, individuals in northern Thailand were literally born into houses; this was before hospital birthing became common. The houses were themselves geographical locations constructed around a sacred center, the "auspicious post" that served as "the ritual center of the dwelling" (Davis 1984, 49).

The inhabitants of the house were guided in their actions and interactions by spirits. When a child was born, his or her identity was immediately established by announcing to the spirits that a new family member had arrived and had become part of the minijurisdiction over which the spirits presided. The elders placed the newborn child on a flat, round bamboo tray for winnowing rice (*kradong*) and asked the household spirits (*phi rüan*) and the ancestral spirits of the family rice pot (*pu dam ya dam*, literally Black Grandfather and Grandmother) to guard and protect the newborn: "Receive this baby as your child; accept this newborn member of our household" (interview with Thipha). Then the baby was taken to the top of the stairs near the entrance to the house, where it was presented to the spirit mother and spirit father (*pho koet mae koet*) with these words: "If this is a human baby, let it live. If it is a spirit baby, then take it away" (Id.). A baby who was born before his or her destined time would return to the world of the spirits and would soon die of a fever or other cause.[8]

The identity of each villager was connected from birth to a specific location and a geographically based community of humans and spirits. Birth rituals were among the "social techniques for the inscription of locality onto bodies" and served to "locate bodies in socially and spatially defined communities" (Appadurai 1996, 179), which were oriented around the sacred centers of house and village. Injuries, illnesses, and other mishaps were located in relation to the sacred centers and the supernatural beings who presided over them. For example, if a baby cried all night or if a child was sick or injured, the family prayed for the intercession of the ancestral spirits of the rice pot, *pu dam ya dam*. The clay rice pot blackened by smoke from burning wood was a prominent feature of the house's kitchen—a "place" in the geography of the home. As one interviewee recalls, the elders would take three balls of sticky rice and place them at the clay cooking stove as an offering. They would then pray, "*Pu dam ya dam*, please protect our children. Watch over our children. Don't let them cry at night" (interview with Kham).

Other household spirits required regular propitiation and notification of the family's comings and goings. In exchange, they offered protection against harm: "If you wanted to do anything, you had to consider the household spirits first. They were always watching. People respected them" (interview with Bancha). Villagers propitiated the spirits and asked for their protection on special occasions such as Songkran Day (traditional Thai New Year), when they presented incense, candles, fruit, and chickens while praying: "Household spirits, please guard and protect us. Look after our house. Keep us from harm. May those who live in this house live in happiness and comfort" (interview with Bancha).

Spirits were involved in many aspects of injury practices. Injuries inflicted on a villager could offend the spirits and require propitiatory ceremonies. If individuals behaved disrespectfully, the spirits themselves could cause injuries as a form of punishment. When illness or injury occurred, moreover, the household spirits had the power not only to relieve suffering but to identify the underlying cause. In one such ritual, the family rice pot was covered with a black, long-sleeved shirt, and two women who were traditional healers sat on either side. They would ask the spirits of the rice pot, "What about this person? Where did he get in trouble? What did he do wrong?" A wooden stick, suspended above a large flat bamboo tray filled with grains of rice, would then swing back and forth as the spirits inscribed their answer in the rice (interview with Mŭang).

Territorial guardian spirits (*jao thi jao thang*) watched over the household (see Wijeyewardene 1970; Terwiel 1976; Rhum 1994; Tanabe 2002), and villagers built shrines to them within each compound. The so-called spirit house is still a familiar feature of most Thai residences—a miniature dwelling, often elevated on a post and positioned outside the house itself. Most interviewees recalled childhood practices associated with these spirits. Each day, their parents would light incense sticks and candles and would offer sweet and savory foods. The household guardian spirits could reveal the cause of an accident or illness and point the household members toward a solution:

> If someone in the house was ill or injured and didn't get better after seeing a doctor, the elders would make an offering at the shrine of the guardian spirits. They would ask the spirits to enter their dreams and explain why the person was suffering and what needed to be done to get better. They would enter the dreams of someone in the house. It might be anyone. And when we dream, they may come and talk with us, "Oh, you went out and a ghost got you, this ghost or that ghost. A ghost of some dead person. (laughs) A ghost of someone with no relatives [i.e. no one to perform the rituals that would allow the ghost to leave the spot where he had died]." . . . If you encountered this type of ghost or failed to show proper respect, if you walked on it or stepped on its head, then you must perform a ceremony to feed it a duck or chicken. (interview with Bancha)

The intimate relationships of the household were enlarged and replicated at the village level. The word for village, *mu ban*, means literally "a group of households." The village chief in northern Thailand is the *pho luang*, or "big father," suggesting a collective familial relationship within the village. Guardian spirits watched over the entire village, just as they watched over each household. These locality spirits were known by many names, such as *pho ban* ("village father") or *jao ban* ("lord of the village"). In one village we visited, the *sŭa ban* ("village ancestral spirits") resided in large, houselike shrines, where the villagers made merit during the Thai New Year or when they got married, built a new house, or had a funeral. To invoke the spirits' protection, villagers offered flowers, whiskey, and food, both sweet and savory, and they prayed: "Today we are having a wedding. Please, help and take care of this couple. Keep them from danger" (interview with Bancha). Failure of a villager or a household to propitiate the village guardian spirit could cause misfortune.

PLATE 3.2 *Double structure housing the guardian spirits of a village in Sanpatong District, Chiangmai. (David M. Engel)*

PLATE 3.3 *Medium in Sanpatong District, Chiangmai, embodying the village guardian spirits to enable direct communication with villagers. (David M. Engel)*

Even Buddhist temples had their own (non-Buddhist) guardian spirits, or *sŭa wat,* which were propitiated by monks and villagers. Rhum (1994, 47) refers to them as "*wat*-protecting spirits." One commentator (Ramitanon 2002, 34) has used the term *villagers' Buddhism* to describe this amalgam of Buddhist and non-Buddhist elements in rural Thai communities. Locality spirits were positioned at the center of village cosmologies that also included Buddhist shrines, temples, monks, and saints.[9]

In short, households and villages were nodes of social and spiritual interconnection. Residence in these communities conferred identity on humans and spirits and gave a place and a meaning to important events, including injuries. The communities were locality based, centering on shrines and sacred markers that symbolized the spatial locus of human and supernatural authority. Identity as a household member and villager arose from participation in rituals affirming the communities of people and spirits, which in turn reproduced the sense of locality constituted around the sacred centers: "The long term reproduction of a neighborhood that is simultaneously practical, valued, and taken-for-granted depends on the seamless interaction of localized spaces and times with local subjects possessed of the knowledge to reproduce locality" (Appadurai 1996, 181).

To understand how injuries were conceptualized and handled within communities established around sacred centers, it is necessary to mention some of the key attributes of identity that were familiar to those who resided there. These identity attributes defined the nature of injury itself—what aspect of a human being was harmed when an injury occurred and what remedy or response was most appropriate for the injury victim and the community as a whole. Particularly relevant to an understanding of injuries were the components of identity known as *khwan* and *winyan.*

The first identity attribute, the *khwan,* is a flighty spiritual essence found in all living beings and in some natural objects such as rice fields and mountains. Even automobiles may have a *khwan.*[10] When an individual suffers fright, trauma, or physical injury, it is said that the *khwan* flies out of the body, and a ritual—known as *riak khwan* or, in northern dialect, *hong khwan*—must then be performed to recall the *khwan*

PLATE 3.4 *Small shrine housing the guardian spirit of the temple (*sŭa wat*), Wat Ton Kwen, Hang Dong District, Chiangmai. (David M. Engel)*

and bind it in the body by tying a sacred string or thread around the wrists. Loss of the *khwan* causes the individual to become unwell, both physically and mentally, and the confusion and alienation of the afflicted person was, at least in the past, understood to pose a risk to the entire community. Symbolically, the lost *khwan* was thought to escape from the physical boundaries of the village and enter a realm beyond that of human society. As Tambiah (1970, 243) writes concerning the *khwan* ceremony in Northeast Thailand:

> [T]he spirit essence is thought of as having gone to that part of the external world which is the very opposite of society and human habitation (village)—the forest, cave, mountain, river—lured there by animals of the forest. . . . In other words, the escape of the spirit essence from an individual is suggestive of the escape of a person from his village and community members and into the forest and its non-human inhabitants. . . . When the elders call the *khwan* and restore it to the body, it is they who are charging the celebrant with the vital social force of morale, and they thus enable the celebrant to accept and bind himself to what is expected of him.

Recalling the *khwan* of an injured person was seen as essential to repair the fabric of the community. Significantly, the payment made by the injurer was—and still is—referred to as "payment for the *khwan* ceremony" (*kha tham khwan*). This term, even today, is widely used in Thai society to describe the compensation that is paid in an injury case. It is understandable that, in the closely integrated village society of humans and spirits, the entire community would insist that the injurer pay compensation. The injurer's transgression put everyone at risk, and the victim would cease to be a functional member of his family and his village until the *khwan* was recalled and bound firmly into the victim's body. Because each injury had this collective aspect, compelling the payment of injury costs was assumed to be essential to the preservation of the village community.

The second component of human identity that is relevant to this discussion of injuries is another type of spiritual essence known as *winyan*. More durable than the *khwan*, the *winyan* leaves the body only at the time of death. Buddhist rituals to make merit for the *winyan* can ensure its progression toward a favorable future life, and ultimately the *winyan* should undergo reincarnation; but when death results from an injury, there is a danger that the *winyan* will remain at the spot of the fatality. When a violent or unnatural death (*tai hong*) occurs, the *winyan* that is allowed to linger at the location becomes the most dangerous type of ghost (*phi tai hong*). It waits until other humans come near to sicken or kill them so that a new *winyan* will take its place and it can continue its normal path in the cycle of birth and rebirth. Thus, when violent or unnatural deaths occur, it is imperative to perform a ritual aimed at preventing this type of dangerous and malevolent ghost from arising.[11] Interviewees recalled that the cost of these merit-making ceremonies in cases of abnormal death was an obligation assumed by the injurer. The entire village had an interest in enforcing this obligation because everyone was put at risk by the dangerous and malevolent *phi tai hong.*

In sum, the remembered law of sacred centers began with traditions located in households and villages. In proximity to those geographical centers, individuals acquired an identity and a status, and they fell under the protection of territorially based authorities—both human and supernatural—who could interpret the cause of injuries, identify the transgressions that caused them, and enforce the payment of compensation. Injuries within the community disrupted social harmony and threatened the well-being of all. The collective interest in redressing this kind of normative violation was voiced by the spirits through various means, such as the ritual to ascertain the views of household spirits and ceremonies associated with spirit mediums, traditional healers, and others. Village elders, including the village or subdistrict chief, served as agents of human authority to compel the payment of compensation. All these practices were understood to be consistent with "villagers' Buddhism," which was actually a heterogeneous mix of Buddhist and non-Buddhist customs and beliefs.

According to Eoseewong (1998, 22–24), the household and village guardian spirits formerly enforced a localized customary law at the village level. When villagers violated social norms, the guardian spirits identified the transgressors and demanded that they be called to account. Eoseewong distinguishes between the ghosts of particular deceased individuals—the *winyan* that linger among humans and cause trouble rather than proceeding on the cycle of rebirth—and the household or

PLATE 3.5 *Tree in Hang Dong District, Chiangmai, in which a spirit resides. Villagers' offerings to contain the spirit are accompanied by Buddhist images and rituals. (David M. Engel)*

village guardian spirits. The latter, according to Eoseewong, were re-garded generically as ancestral spirits but were not associated with any identifiable individual. As nonindividualized beings, they played a key social role. They were not the frightening "ghosts" that, in Eoseewong's view, became part of Thai folklore relatively recently. Rather, they were the respected upholders of social norms and customs. In particular, the locality-based guardian spirits were the enforcers of a village-level cus-tomary law concerning injury and compensation.

Injury and Identity in the Forest

As recalled by the interviewees in this study, the prototypical law of sacred centers was the localized customary legal order associated with the house and village. Space was conceived as radiating outward from these centers—and from the guardian spirits and markers around which the centers were constructed. Their potency weakened as individuals moved farther from them—across the fields, into the forests, and onto the high-ways leading to other villages and towns. Injuries located at a distance were less likely to result in compensation to the victim. Of course, other vil-lages, towns, and provinces also had their own sacred centers. Yet for each person one particular locality had special significance—the one where he or she was "registered" with the guardian spirits and familiar with the local norms and authority figures. Outside this locality, unless the person had reregistered with spirits elsewhere, legal enforcement became problematic.

Beyond the village and the rice fields, and in some cases directly adjacent to them, the dense forests and mountains of northern Thailand represented zones of ambiguity and risk. Unlike the village, the forest was unregulated by customary law. It was wild and uncivilized. Injuries in the forest, it seemed, were nearly always caused by dangerous spirits who lived beyond the boundaries of civilization. Such spirits could be offended by improper human behavior, even when it was inadvertent, and in retaliation they could inflict injury or illness or could cause the transgressor to become hopelessly lost. Stepping on or climbing a tree occupied by a spirit could lead to unfortunate results, but most often mishaps occurred because villagers urinated or defecated in the for-est without asking permission of the spirits. If the spot they chose was

PLATE 3.6 *View of rice fields, forests, and mountains in Chiangdao District, Chiangmai. (David M. Engel)*

occupied by a spirit, they were likely to suffer retaliation, sometimes in the form of an accident that might appear superficially to be the fault of another person.

Injury and death in the forest were seldom blamed on the misdeeds of the human injurers who ostensibly caused them. Our interviewees nearly always attributed such injuries to the forest spirits—and to the victim him- or herself, who had failed to show respect to the spirits. Thus, one villager told us that he always prayed to the guardian spirits of the forest before he entered, to ward off danger. Moreover, he was careful to speak properly in the forest, not to tell jokes or falsehoods, and to use proper language so he would not offend the spirits. If he wished to sleep in the forest, he would have to ask permission of the spirits before building a sleeping platform in a tree. Otherwise, the spirit would send a vision in the night causing him to think that the rope used to construct the platform was actually a poisonous centipede. Hacking frantically at the imagined centipede, he could cut through the rope and fall to his death. Such were the injuries that the forest spirits could inflict on humans who failed to respect and propitiate them (interview with Kham).

Forest spirits could also cause humans to become hopelessly lost and die without finding their way home. This could occur if a person stepped over a type of vine called *khrüa khao long* (literally the "go-astray vine"). The spirits would retaliate for this transgression by making the person unable to recognize the path leading out of the forest. A human wandering lost in the forest might meet a ghost who greeted him by name. Under no circumstances should the greeting be acknowledged, because the ghost, on verifying the human's name, could cause him or her to go deeper and deeper into the forest without hope of finding the way out. The proper response to a stranger's greeting in the forest was either to make a grunt or other sound or to imitate the call of an owl. Any of these responses would keep people safe and prevent them from getting lost.

Although some people entered the forest to hunt or collect forest products, others sought more aggressively to tame or destroy the forest. The forest lands of northern Thailand are now crisscrossed by major highways. Those who constructed the highways were at special risk of injury or death as they cut down thousands of trees and destroyed the natural habitat for human purposes. For smaller projects, construction workers performed a ceremony to propitiate the forest spirits and promised to offer them a chicken, duck, or pig's head once the work was finished. But for large-scale highway construction, such offerings were insufficient. Unless the spirits were offered an actual human life, construction workers might be injured or killed. Therefore, the spirits were told that when the project was completed they would be free to select as a sacrifice any victim from among those who were to travel on the highway through the spirits' domain in the forest:

> When you built a new highway, you didn't sacrifice a chicken or a duck or any animal; you sacrificed a person. You offered a person's head. They left it to the spirits to choose a person who had come to the end of his karma and whose time had come to die. If it's not a person's time, he won't die. That's how it is. (interview with Jampa)

Highway accidents that might appear to result from the negligence of another human were, according to these customary beliefs and practices, actually rooted in the actions of the spirits of the forest; but the Buddhist concept of karma also played a part by determining whose prior misdeeds made them vulnerable. The spirits of the forest were not benevolent like the ancestral spirits located in households and villages, nor did they enforce customary legal systems that provided compensation to injury victims. They were uncivilized and frightening. Stories of injuries in the forest did not emphasize the transgressions of other human actors but only of the victims themselves, who had offended the forest spirits or failed to propitiate them before entering their territory. Responsibility for such injuries rested on the persons who omitted the proper rituals of respect and protection or were remiss in performing the usual merit-making ceremonies to maintain a healthy karmic balance. Such individuals were primarily responsible for suffering harm at the hands of the spirits who presided over this dangerous portion of the landscape.

Injury and Identity Far from Home

The weakening of the law of sacred centers became more pronounced as individuals traveled farther from home, toward other villages and towns. The highways themselves could be a source of danger because the malevolent ghosts of accident victims resided along the roadside. When injuries occurred on the highway, the cause was often traced back to the depredations of these ghosts, known as *phi tai hong*. Such ghosts could obscure the vision of a person who came too close or could otherwise try to cause a fatal accident in order to have the victim's *winyan* take the place of the ghost and allow the latter to leave that location and resume its spiritual progression toward a new birth. Such explanations did not necessarily support the assumption that the injured person should receive customary compensation from another human, because the essence of the problem was the ghost rather than the injurer.

The fear of *phi tai hong* made it essential to perform proper rituals (*sut thon*) at the place where an abnormal death occurred. Buajan's injury narrative in Chapter 1 provides a description of this ceremony, but other interviewees presented different variations. Kham, for example, recalled that monks who performed the ritual placed the *winyan* in a bamboo fish trap to remove it from the place where it had fallen at the time of death. He remembered that the lightweight fish trap became extremely heavy once the officiants placed the added weight of the malevolent ghost inside, and it took four men to lift it and carry it away to be buried at the foot of a sacred bo tree in the cemetery outside a temple.

As we saw in Buajan's narrative, the *sut thon* ritual also involved the placement of miniature sand stupas at the spot where the accident occurred, along with small flags made from colored paper. Bancha remembers a slightly different version of the same ritual involving an offering tray filled with sweets and small clay animals, which the officiants placed in the river at the conclusion of the ceremony and allowed to float away:

> They make an offering tray from a banana tree. They measure the forearm of the person who was killed and make a square tray the same size as his forearm. Then they make decorations from betel leaves, sugar cane, and banana, and there's also rice, butter cakes, and so on. They take plasticine or clay and make into the shape of all different types of animals, such as chickens, pigs, and water buffalo. They make all of these into tiny animal shapes. Then, when the *sut thon* ceremony is finished, they carry the tray to the river and float it in the water. When it is floating, then the officiant will perform his own ritual with flowers and so forth. He will

PLATE 3.7 *Bamboo fish traps similar to that which was said by Kham to have been used to carry a malevolent ghost (*phi tai hong*) from the site of a fatality to its burial place beneath a bo tree. (David M. Engel)*

scatter the flowers on the water and light candles. He will make a vow and chant sacred words of his own, and he will blow on the tray. They believe that the *winyan* should float away on the water so it can be free. It can die and reach the end of its journey. It won't come back anymore to seek vengeance and repeat the karmic cycle. Let it float away with the water currents.

Whatever the precise details of the *sut thon* ceremony, villagers believed that it had to be performed to prevent one fatality from leading to other injuries and deaths. The ceremony was associated with a customary law of injuries in that its costs were regarded as the responsibility of the injurer and provided a measure of the compensation to which the victim or the family was entitled. But injuries and fatalities far from home presented another problem: the difficulty of negotiating a remedy. When the claimant and injurer lived in the same village, the village chief or subdistrict chief (*kamnan*) could remind them of the norms and expectations for paying compensation after an injury took place. Because both parties worshipped the same guardian spirits, they were literally brothers and sisters who had to treat one another with respect and generosity. But when injuries occurred on the highway, the disputants were likely to have been strangers to one another and may have found themselves without a mutually acceptable mediator. In such cases, injurers who disagreed about their obligation to pay for the *sut thon* ceremony might discover that there was no authority figure to compel them to change their minds. In legal spaces where authority radiates outward from a sacred center, the more distant a location is from the center that holds significance for the disputants the more problematic enforcement becomes.

Injuries off the Map: Delocalized Causes of Harm

We have spoken thus far of injuries that were associated with specific locations: the house, the village, the forest, and the highway. Yet even in the imagined landscape familiar to preceding generations, many causes of injury were not locality based and could not be mapped at all. For example, karmic explanations of injury, which often appeared in combination with other explanations, were not place specific. They referred to the injured person's own misdeeds, either in this life or in an earlier life. The injury was thus a consequence of actions the injury victim had previously directed at the injurer or at another person or even an animal—as in Buajan's injury narrative. The effects of these actions later manifested themselves in the form of an accident.

Karmic explanations placed the ultimate causal responsibility on the victim him- or herself. What then of the injurer? A different type of explanation that may be more common in the present than in the past is negligence. The concept of negligence is also "off the map" in that its causal roots are not fixed to any particular geographical location. The Thai word for "negligent" is *pramat* (careless, imprudent), which is also a legal term, but its colloquial meaning in Thai carries some connotations that are lacking in English. When individuals cited the injurer's negligence as one cause of their injury, they usually hastened to add that they themselves had also been negligent. Negligence on the part of both parties—injured and injurer—appear to be linked conceptually in the minds of ordinary people in Thailand.

Injuries occurred because both parties lacked *sati*, or mindfulness. *Sati* is another Buddhist concept, signifying a mind that is focused, calm, aware, and undistracted.[12] *Sati* can be achieved through concentration and meditation as well as a philosophical understanding of the illusory quality of everyday life. Negligence is, in a sense, the opposite of *sati*: "[I]f you are negligent then you don't have *sati*; you are acting without *sati*" (interview with Suwit). The concept of negligence was thus closely connected to the concept we might call "contributory negligence," and both in turn were tied to the Buddhist concept of an undisciplined mind[13] and a lack of spiritual training and awareness. Moreover, the teachings of the Buddha would explain that negligence was a secondary cause of injury, not the root cause. The root cause, from a Buddhist perspective, is karma. The carelessness of both parties and their lack of *sati* have karmic origins.

Karma and negligence were two of the most important "off-the-map" causal explanations for injuries. Neither cause has specific spatial referents; neither has a geographic "place." Interviewees also identified other nonlocalized explanations for injury. The concept of fate or destiny (*khro*), for example, is connected to karma yet distinguishable from it. Women "have *khro*" when their age is an odd number, but men have *khro*, and are therefore more susceptible to injury, when their age is an even number. According to Keyes (1977, 117), *khro* is a non-Buddhist concept of causation "that operates irrespective of the moral actions of people, whereas the Buddhist concept of Karma relates all causation ultimately to moral action." Nevertheless, injury victims in northern Thailand tended to merge the two concepts in a single expression, *khrokam*, and they spoke of their *khro* as the product of bad karma they had accumulated through misdeeds in their current or previous lifetimes. We have seen this conflation of karma and *khro* in the injury narrative of Buajan in Chapter 1.

Injuries sometimes arose from another nonlocalized cause, one's "stars" (*duang*). When a person's stars are in the ascendancy, good luck of all kinds may occur—one may win the lottery, succeed in gambling, and achieve success in all endeavors. But when one's stars are on the decline, bad fortune is likely, and injuries may occur.

Injuries could even be caused by a person's name. One interviewee, for example, complained that his parents did not give him a name that was appropriate for the day, month, and year of his birth. An inappropriate name can bring bad luck and make one susceptible to injuries. At the time of the interview, he was considering a name change to improve his luck and avoid further mishaps. A female interviewee, Saikham, changed her name after her husband was killed in a traffic accident, but this did not protect her several years later from a motorcycle collision that broke her leg. It may, however, have made her accident less serious and saved her life.

All of these delocalized causes of injury—karma, negligence, absence of *sati*, fate, stars, and other forms of bad luck—had one thing in common: None of them, except perhaps the injurer's negligence, was associated with a remedy of any kind, or at least a remedy that the injurer was obliged to provide. If the cause of the injury was the victim's own karma, contributory negligence, lack of *sati*, fate, or bad luck, then why should the injurer take responsibility? In the past, these delocalized causal explanations were familiar and widely accepted, yet they did not necessarily relieve the injurer of an obligation to pay compensation. When injuries occurred in villages near the watchful eyes of the guardian spirits, the delocalized explanations were rarely regarded as the *exclusive* cause of the injury. Causation was multiple, shifting, and overlapping.

No single explanation trumped the others. All of them were relevant, and combinations of them were likely to be mentioned when an injury occurred. The village chief could refer to the victim's karma at the same time that he reminded the injurer that he or she had violated local norms and disturbed the well-being of the entire village. Injuries could be simultaneously localized and delocalized. In the normal course of things, injurers were in the end expected to pay compensation.

Conclusion

In this chapter, we have described two different systems of law that could address the problem of injury in northern Thailand. The state law of injuries has been in place since the early twentieth century and rests on the distinctive geopolitical mappings and ideologies that are characteristic of the nation-state. The law of sacred centers predated the advent of state law but is now in decline. In our research, we had access to it primarily through the recollections of our interviewees as they described the mapping of space and the beliefs and practices they had learned from their parents and grandparents. This concept of legality still has relevance in the present, but, as the next chapter describes, it has been radically transformed by recent changes in Thai society.

Sacred centers—such as pillars, trees, shrines, mountains, or locations associated with ghosts—were of paramount importance to villagers but were not recognized by state law. In making the physical and social landscape "legible," according to Scott (1998, 80), the state must simplify what it sees, and "state simplifications are observations of only those aspects of social life that are of official interest." Ghosts and spirits, which were central to customary law in Thailand, were of no official interest. They were not "seen" by the modern Thai state.

For ordinary Thais, these two imaginings of the landscape of injury might seem to present a conflict. From the perspective of the state, injuries were mapped according to the administrative unit in which they occurred. All injuries were subject to national laws, both civil and criminal. State law's penalties and procedures for injuries corresponded imperfectly at best to the consequences for violating customary laws or the procedures by which customary law was applied. Yet these two types of legality had in fact accommodated to one another in many ways throughout the twentieth century. The village chief who mediated injury cases acted not only as a lower-level government official but also as a spokesperson for customary legal norms. The outcomes he facilitated were traditional remedies conceptualized in terms of the injurer's obligation to pay for Buddhist and spirit-based ceremonies and for recalling the *khwan* soul to the body of the injury victim. Even when injured persons appeared to step outside the system of customary norms and procedures by filing a claim in the provincial court, their typical aim was to obtain a customary remedy. Litigation in such cases did not indicate a rejection of the law of sacred centers but a realization that customary negotiations had reached an impasse. By bringing the claim to court, the injured person hoped to break the impasse. As soon as a traditional injury payment was obtained, the lawsuit was withdrawn (see Engel 1978; 2005). Although resort to state law exposed social relationships to new concepts of legal rights and rationalized procedures, it also represented a merger of the two types of legality. State law reinforced customary law by serving as a forum of last resort in the quest for a traditional remedy; customary law legitimated state law by incorporating it into a view of the world that was familiar to ordinary people.

State law was in many ways alien, distant, and threatening. It was to be avoided if possible, and those who invoked state law often came to regret it. Yet a small number of injury cases made their way to the provincial court each year, as court records from the 1960s and 1970s demonstrate (Engel 1978; 2005). In those relatively rare instances, the two types of legality operated in a mutually constitutive fashion, and state law intersected—at least fleetingly—with customary law. As the next chapter will suggest, by the end of the twentieth century, such points of intersection had all but disappeared.

4

Injury Practices in a Transformed Society

> I remember our village near the forest in
> the highlands more than forty years ago.
> In those days they said that the moun-
> tains and forests and rural towns were
> full of spirits. The old people told us that
> there were spirits in every blade of grass.
> Over the entire surface of the earth, you
> could not find any place larger than the
> palm of your hand that was free of spirits.
>
> *Mala Khamchan (2001, 27–28)*

> It is unfortunate that the Thai people
> have abandoned their belief in spirits, but
> we have not established in their place a
> system of law and legal institutions that
> are considered sacred. We have lost the
> spirits and gained nothing in exchange.
>
> *Nidhi Eoseewong (1998, 25)*

THE PRECEDING CHAPTER PRESENTED TWO MAPS of the landscape of injury in northern Thailand, one associated with state law and the other with the law of sacred centers. Previously, the two maps co-existed and interacted in relatively predictable ways. Neither supplanted the other, and individuals who had been injured could draw on both types of legality to frame their experiences and seek a remedy. Occasionally, injured persons would even follow a pathway from the law of sacred centers to the institutions of state law.

Interconnections of this kind between two types of legality are not surprising and in fact are predicted by sociolegal theory. Santos (1995,

464), in his own description of legal mapping, refers to such connections as "interlegality": "[O]ne cannot properly speak of law and legality, but rather of interlaw and interlegality. More important than the identification of the different legal orders is tracing the complex and changing relations among them." The state's mapping of law within fixed geopolitical boundaries is never complete. "Modern" law is never fully disconnected from its cultural context or, as in the case of Thailand, from maps based on the sacred centers of customary law. Indeed, as Fitzpatrick (2007, 157) has observed, for law to function effectively it *depends* on its interactions with sacred elements in the culture despite its claims to transcendence and autonomy: "The combined presence and denial of the sacred go to form modern law operatively."

Interlegality in Thailand was apparent in the injury cases that came to the Chiangmai Provincial Court in the 1960s and 1970s. Many contained internal evidence of a failure in the village-level customary law procedures. Mediation by village leaders could fail for many reasons: The accident may have occurred far from home, where no mediator could command the acquiescence of both parties; the two parties could come from different villages, and distance could frustrate the mediation process; one of the parties might him- or herself be a person of high status or authority who refused to submit to the intervention of a locally based third party (Engel 1978, 137–149). When the mediation process broke down, the Provincial Court represented a forum of last resort. No injurer could defy the authority of the Court, which was understood to act in the name of the king. Plaintiffs typically used the court to obtain customary remedies through out-of-court settlements, and they withdrew their suit as soon as the defendant paid an amount that was measured not by the requirements of the law codes but by the cost of performing traditional rituals to propitiate the spirits, recall the lost *khwan*, or make merit for the *winyan* of the deceased.

Litigation, as it appeared in our earlier research in Chiangmai, was rare but consistent with locality-based compensation systems. It was viewed as legitimate because it helped individuals to obtain customary remedies, and litigation in turn reinforced such practices by reinstitutionalizing them at the state level. To this extent, formal law was linked to customary practices in a mutually legitimizing relationship.

After the socioeconomic transformations of the 1980s and 1990s, however, these linkages and interconnections became more difficult to sustain. Villagers lived and worked far from home. They interacted frequently with strangers. Traditional mediators lost their authority. Local communities broke apart as young people left for the cities and farm land was bought by developers and other entrepreneurs. Such demographic and socioeconomic changes resulted in a loss of authority by local spirits and leaders. The connections between on-the-map and off-the-map perceptions of injuries were severed. At the same time, the mutually reinforcing linkages between locality-based dispute resolution and litigation in the Provincial Court were shattered. Resort to official law by injury victims lost its legitimacy and became even more rare than in the past.

Global changes at the end of the twentieth century, then, have been accompanied by a reduction of "interlegality" in injury cases almost to the vanishing point. Although one might expect injured persons to turn increasingly to state law for the remedy that customary law can no longer provide, we shall see in Chapter 5 that this has proved not to be the case. None of the interviewees in our study used or perceived state law in this way. None consulted a lawyer in response to the injury. None even expressed the view that compensation for injuries should be mandated by the Thai judicial system. It appears that the court is used *less frequently* per injury today than in the past.[1]

In this chapter, we shift our focus from a landscape of injuries that our interviewees associated with the past to the landscape of the present. We ask how the social changes experienced in Thailand during the last decades of the twentieth century led to a transformation of the map of sacred centers and of the "interlegality" that connected it to the official legal system. We will describe the effects of these changes in terms of the *relocalization* and the *delocalization* of injuries. Injuries have tended to become "relocalized" in the sense that the site of the event is understood to be a place that is distant from the village community in which the victim was born and was given an identity. Injuries have become "delocalized" in the sense that their off-the-map qualities are viewed as much more significant than their connection to the place where they occur. Both the relocalization and delocalization of injuries disrupt the attribution of responsibility to another person. Instead, injuries are considered the responsibility of the injured person, who is expected to provide his or her own protection from harm and to pay his or her own injury costs.

Relocalization of Injury

As a result of the socioeconomic transformations of the late twentieth century, people in northern Thailand tend to live and travel away from their birth communities. Consequently, injuries no longer occur near a sacred center that is known and respected by both the injurer and the victim. Most injuries now occur far from home, near other less familiar centers or outside the reach of any form of customary ordering. In only one instance did an interviewee describe an injury located in the village where he was born. In that case, local customary practices were applicable, and mediation by a village leader was still possible. More typically, however, injuries are not viewed as a matter of collective concern to the humans and spirits in a particular location. There is no community that demands a resolution. Loss of the *khwan* no longer has implications for the rest of the village, and behavior that injures the individual no longer offends the guardian spirits. Compensation obtained or not obtained from the injurer to restore the physical, psychological, and spiritual well-being of the injured person no longer affects others who live nearby. There is no village leader of whom the disputants can say, in the words of one of our interviewees, "He knows the accused, and he knows the accuser. He knows both of them. He will do justice to both of them" (interview with Manit).

The relocalization of injuries is partly a by-product of population movement in northern Thailand. Because individuals spend less time in their birth villages, it is more likely that the injuries they suffer will occur in distant locales. More broadly, however, relocalization is connected to a weakening of the ties between individuals and the sacred centers that formerly shaped identities and daily practices. When babies are born today, they are less likely to be presented to the local guardian spirits because births increasingly take place in hospitals rather than homes. Birth rituals are less often performed, and children do not immediately become a part of the community of humans and spirits as they did in the past. Similarly, when young people marry in hotels rather than in their home village, the traditional wedding ceremonies no longer resemble the community celebrations of the past, and the new spouse does not necessarily move in with the parents and grandparents or "register" with the household spirits as a new member of the family. Instead, young couples often live and work in the city and not in the villages where they were raised. In these and other ways, the linkages between individuals and sacred centers have been weakened. The relocalization of injury is symptomatic of a more general loss of locality-based identity in northern Thailand.

The narratives we obtained in our interviews offer abundant evidence of the relocalization of injury. Buajan's story (Chapter 1) is a typical example. She lived and worked in the city far from her birth village. Her accident occurred near a food stall along the highway in a location that had no particular significance for her or her injurer. Although a malevolent ghost may have been one of the causes of the accident, there was no sacred center in the proximity that was known to Buajan or the old man who ran over her. No guardian spirits were offended by the incident. No community of spirits and humans demanded a remedy.

The process of relocalization in such cases places the incident far from any sacred center that the parties associate with a viable system of customary law. Injury victims still recalled the mapping of injury and identity that had been familiar to their parents, but those maps no longer served as reliable guides. Because injuries are relocalized outside the reach of any customary legal system that the parties could use, there is little possibility that another human actor might be named responsible for the injury and required to pay compensation. It is now up to individuals to protect themselves as best they can by exercising caution and by attending to matters of karma and good or bad fortune.

With the weakening of sacred centers of authority and customary law, traditional mediators and respected elders have experienced an erosion of authority when disputes arise. Village leaders now turn away injury victims, telling them that they lack jurisdiction over incidents occurring outside the village or that they cannot mediate unless the injurer and the victim both reside in the same locale. In the past, the village chief and *kamnan* were uniquely situated to dispense justice *because* they were locally based. As Manit observed, the village chief could tell the disputants, "We are fellow villagers. Let's compromise. Let's try to understand each other a little." Such interventions were likely to achieve

justice precisely because the mediator knew the disputants well and because the roles and identities of all the actors were defined by the locality
of which they were a part. When the dispute is resolved by a stranger—a
police officer or a judge—the case can easily be turned around, right can
be made to seem wrong, and the culpable injurer can be made to appear
innocent. In Manit's words,

> If we go to the court, they don't know us. Just like you, professor, or the
> doctors here in the hospital, you don't know me. If I go to the court, al-
> though I do respect it, who is right and who is wrong is up to them. The
> decisions of some courts, well . . . But the village chief and the *kamnan*
> know who I am. They know the accused, and they know the accuser.
> They know both of them. They will do justice to both of them.

The process of relocalization has therefore made it more difficult to
achieve fair compensation at the same time that it has redefined the parties at interest. The significance of injuries for a broader community has
been lost, customary remediation procedures have become irrelevant,
and local mediators have been disempowered.

Delocalization of Injury

The second transformation of the landscape of injuries involves the
pervasive tendency to view injuries in terms of their *delocalized* qualities. That is, the causes that are "off the map"—karma, fate, stars—have
become highly significant in the perceptions of injury victims, and injuries are often viewed as lacking any locational significance whatsoever.
Malevolent ghosts (*phi tai hong*) are still thought to cause injuries in
particularly risky places, but when injuries occur far from the view of
village guardian spirits, their mapping becomes less consequential and
therefore of less interest to the parties. Emphasis on the delocalized aspects of an injury—in particular, a predominant emphasis on its karmic
origins—contributes to the failure of customary law and makes the issue
of compensation problematic or even irrelevant.

The delocalization of injuries—the tendency to offer explanations
that cannot be mapped—may be part of a broader shift in the ontology
of Thai belief systems. As we have seen, "villagers' Buddhism" in the past

integrated Buddhist and animist beliefs and practices into a seamless whole. Belief in karma and other aspects of formal Buddhist doctrine existed side by side with belief in local guardian spirits, *khwan*, and *winyan*. Put another way, villagers' Buddhism contained both locality-based and delocalized elements. These elements were not sharply distinguished, for there was no need to do so. Phenomena—including injuries—could be explained simultaneously in terms of karma, fate, and locality spirits. But as individuals tend increasingly to live and work far from home, they have less opportunity to propitiate village guardian spirits, to inform them of their activities, and to seek their protection and guidance. The delocalized aspects of injury have separated from the localized aspects.

Observers of contemporary Thai society have noted an enormous growth in the popularity of what we might call delocalized deities, who can affect human lives but are not tied to a particular spatial location or sacred center. Such deities have, in a sense, replaced village-based sacred places and entities, both Buddhist and non-Buddhist. One is *jao mae kuan im*, a female godlike figure of Chinese origin who is associated with morality, piety, and kindness (Ganjanapan 2002, 131).[2] Images of *jao mae kuan im* can now be seen throughout Thailand, and interviewees often mentioned her as an object of veneration. Equally ubiquitous is King Rama V, known by his abbreviation as *ro ha* ("R 5"). Long respected as a shrewd and able ruler who steered his country past the shoals of colonialism into an era of independence and "modernity," *ro ha* has in recent years attained godlike status. His pictures and statues are placed on shrines and worshipped in many houses and business establishments throughout the country. As the modernizing king, he is thought to bring "luck in business as well as protection" to those who honor him (Id., 130–131).

Failure to propitiate and worship both *jao mae kuan im* and *ro ha* could bring misfortune, which in turn may lead to injury. Yet, unlike the village and household guardian spirits, these newer deities are delocalized. Their influence and protection is not associated with a particular place. They can be "accessed" wherever people might go as they travel far from their birth village to live and work in Thailand's new economy. Religiosity has become less place dependent.

Other deities or protective spirits are equally mobile and, in some cases, are adopted specifically because they are believed to provide

PLATE 4.1 *Statue of* jao mae kuan im, *the "goddess of mercy," at Wat Phrathat Doi Chom Thong, Amphur Muang, Chiangrai. (David M. Engel)*

PLATE 4.2 *Amulet with image of Rama V (King Chulalongkorn), popularly known and venerated as* ro ha *and thought to provide prosperity and protection to those who pray to him. (Nayada Jirampaikool)*

protection as people move from one location to another. Mobile spirits, as opposed to sacred centers, are particularly useful to those who participated in the internal migrations associated with Thailand's economy in the late twentieth century. For example, a pair of "spirit brothers" (*nong kuman*) played a key role in the injury narrative of a young woman named Dao. When Dao was thirteen, poverty forced her mother to send her away from their small village in central Thailand to live with relatives hundreds of miles to the north. Before Dao left on her journey, her mother presented her with the two spirit brothers. These supernatural boys, probably metal or ceramic images, were only a little younger than Dao herself and came originally from her uncle, who was a spirit medium. He gave them to Dao's parents so that they would be prosperous and "live well." He told them that the boys would bring good fortune but that they must take proper care of them: "If we don't feed them, we will suffer" (interview with Dao).

PLATE 4.3 *Small figure of* nong kuman thong, *similar to the spirit brothers to whom Dao made daily offerings of food and sweets. (David M. Engel)*

Dao speaks to the spirit brothers frequently. Each day she offers them fruit, rice, sweet drinks or milk, and occasionally a toy. If she forgets to feed them, they will remind her while she sleeps:

> If I come home from the shop and go straight to bed, they will enter my dreams and ask for something to eat. I tell them to get food for themselves, but they are only spirits, right? How could they find food for themselves? So I have to leave something for them.

Dao must also inform the spirit brothers about her comings and goings before she leaves the house. If she tells them everything, they will protect her. Once they even helped her buy a winning lottery ticket. But if she fails to inform them before she goes out, she will lose their protection with potentially disastrous consequences. That is one of the most important causes of a serious injury she suffered in a motorcycle accident:

> When I left the house, I wasn't thinking about anything. Usually I would tell the spirit brothers, "I'm going to help Older Sister sell things." As soon as I return, I tell them. . . . I tell them every time, but that time I didn't tell them—before the accident happened.

Dao's narrative illustrates how delocalized supernatural figures have replaced village-based spirits in the everyday lives of many Thai citizens. Worshiping such figures can bring good luck and protection. Failing to worship them can bring loss of protection and injury. But these mobile, delocalized spirits do not provide access to any official or unofficial legal system that would require the payment of compensation when injuries occur.

In sum, both the relocalization and delocalization of injuries entail a subtle but highly significant shift in the conceptualization of why injuries occur and what should be done about them. Together, they tend to reduce or eliminate the role played by the law of sacred centers. They make it less likely than ever before that any system of customary law will hold the injurer responsible and require the payment of compensation to the injury victim. Instead, they reinforce interpretations of injury that place the ultimate responsibility for accident prevention on the victim him- or herself.

The Delocalization of Karma

The lowland peoples of northern Thailand are overwhelmingly Buddhist,[3] and belief in the law of karma is central to their religious outlook. Yet the recent social transformations have brought a marked change in the role karma plays in explaining injuries and shaping the responses of injured persons in contemporary Thailand. Buddhism was, of course, a key consideration for injured persons twenty-five years ago and long before that. Yet in the past villagers did not perceive sharp distinctions between their Buddhist beliefs and remediation systems founded on customary village-based practices, spirit worship, and mediation. Mediation of injury cases by secular authority figures also incorporated Buddhist norms of moderation, selflessness, and forgiveness. Buddhism may have tempered the quest for a remedy by discouraging selfish or overly aggressive responses, but it was not understood to prohibit entirely the demand for compensation. Because compensation reflected the interests of the entire village, not just the interests of the injured party, it could be pursued without violating Buddhist precepts. In this sense, Buddhism and belief in karma were viewed as consistent with spirit-based belief systems and the customary law associated with them.

In recent years, however, the integration of Buddhism with other locality-based belief and remediation systems has begun to break down. As individuals leave their birth communities, they worship at temples in locations where they have no network of friends and relations. Indeed, they may have no affiliation with any particular temple, and for ceremonial purposes they may regard a number of temples in various locations as equally suitable. Furthermore, individuals in contemporary Thailand now have access to Buddhism in new and sometimes unprecedented ways, thanks to dramatic technological changes over the past quarter-century. The teachings of charismatic Buddhist teachers have long been available through books, pamphlets, magazines, and newspapers, and nowadays such writings are extremely popular. But new media have facilitated other forms of delocalized Buddhist practice. Televangelism now supplements the ever-popular radio broadcasts of Buddhist sermons. Individuals can also have access to Buddhism over the Internet and by CDs, DVDs, and cassette tapes (compare Hirschkind 2006 on Islamic cassette sermons in Egypt). Devout Buddhists can, and increasingly do, perceive their religious practices as delocalized. Buddhist practices have tended to lose the geographical specificity and the linkage to other localized spirit-based belief systems that they once had.

The accounts of numerous injury victims illustrate the extent to which the Buddhist perspective on injury has been delocalized—cut loose from its geographical anchor in village society. These individuals portrayed their injuries as primarily the result of their own misdeeds. We may recall that Buajan (Chapter 1) believed her broken leg was caused by a wrong she committed years before when she beat and broke the leg of a dog that had entered her house. Others explained that they must have injured their injurer in a previous lifetime, creating karma that had caught up with them in their present life. The cycle of injury and response would continue across many lifetimes, according to the law of karma, unless one of the parties manifested the Buddhist virtues of generosity, compassion, and forgiveness. Consider, for example, the following illustrations in which two men who had suffered injuries, Prayat and Aran, stated that their belief in karma completely precluded remedy seeking and the use of official laws or legal institutions.

Prayat, an agricultural extension worker whose motorcycle was struck by a car, attributed his serious injuries to his own karma. The other driver visited Prayat in the hospital and accepted total responsibility, yet Prayat refused to accept any payment from him or even to file the papers that would provide payment by the other driver's insurance company. Although Prayat considered the other driver negligent, he thought it ultimately a matter of karma. Prayat acknowledged that he did not receive justice and that it may be better for people to invoke the law, but he characterized himself as typical of the people of northern Thailand who prefer to accept the consequences of their own karma rather than vindicate their rights.

Aran is a young, accident-prone restaurant worker who came to the city of Chiangmai from a village background. His fractured knee required surgery following a motorcycle accident in which a teenaged girl cut in front of him. She and her father apologized and promised to pay all the costs for lost wages, medical treatment, and repairs to his motorcycle, but after Aran's surgery they disappeared and paid him nothing. Through the restaurant where Aran works, he has access to a health insurance plan that covered his hospital bills. Aran refused to pursue the possibility of additional compensation by filing a civil or criminal case against the other driver. He believed that he suffers frequent injuries because of the bad karma he accumulated when he killed animals while working in a slaughterhouse. His mother finally made him stop and find other employment, but Aran thought he had not used up his bad karma yet. His wife was later unfaithful to him, and she took his motorcycle and deserted him after his injury, but he forgave her. Aran feared that if he were to pursue a legal remedy against the teenaged girl who injured him in this case, karma might cause his own daughter to encounter some accident or misfortune when she became a teenager. He was unwilling to subject her to this risk, and he chose to protect his daughter by forgiving his injurer in accordance with Buddhist teachings. Aran believed that the other driver and her father will someday suffer the karmic consequences of their misdeeds and their broken promise to provide compensation. It was, therefore, better for everyone if Aran allowed the law of karma to produce justice in the long term rather than seeking a legal remedy in the short term.

These examples, and many others like them, suggest that, in the minds of injured people in contemporary Thailand, their religious belief now precludes the assiduous pursuit of a remedy. The law of karma has come to be positioned in opposition to the law of courts and lawyers. This is a new way of thinking about religion, which was formerly understood to be integrated with village-level beliefs and practices that justified—and to some degree required—the search for compensation and was consistent with the relatively rare use of the Provincial Court for leverage to compel a negotiated settlement of injury claims.

Moreover, karmic explanations of injuries have expanded because people believe that the conditions of modern life make them more vulnerable to injuries caused by karma. As one interviewee observed, a devout Buddhist who has trained him- or herself to be mindful (to have *sati*) at all times can, to some extent, guard against the accidents that karma might otherwise produce. But in contemporary Thai society, it is more difficult than before to maintain *sati*. Both the injurer and the injury victim are hurried, distracted, and careless. Under these circumstances, their karma is far more likely to catch up with them and to manifest itself through the negligence of both parties:

> The factors that cause them to lose *sati* or to be negligent have to do with the way people live their lives everyday at the present time. . . . In today's way of life, people are more likely to be inattentive. Their minds are not at peace. There are so many things that incite and arouse them. They want to go roaming about. They want to have fun. And that makes people lose their *sati*. They do everything fast and carelessly without thinking first. Or they want lots of money, and that can also make them lose their *sati* (interview with Suwit).

In contemporary Thailand, people find it more difficult to maintain the spiritual discipline necessary to guard against karmically induced injury. These same societal changes have transformed the concept of karma itself by removing it from the context of "villagers' Buddhism" and disconnecting it from any functioning system of compensation that an injury victim might attempt to invoke. With the atrophy of customary mechanisms for compensation, and with the relocalization of injuries far from the traditional sacred centers and the delocalization of injuries off the map entirely, injured persons look to themselves and their immediate family to manage their physical and spiritual recovery.

The Individuation of Injury

The processes of relocalization and delocalization have had a profound effect on perceptions and practices in injury cases. As we have seen, injured people increasingly perceive an oppositional relationship between law and their religious beliefs and practices. In addition, injuries have become individuated. The very concept of an injury and the identity of the person who suffers it have undergone a transformation. The loss of the *khwan*, for example, has always been, in some sense, an individualized, delocalized occurrence, yet within the village it can be seen as holding great significance for an entire geographically specific community. In the village context, as we have seen, the *khwan* is said to fly away to the nearby forest. The weakened or dysfunctional individual whose *khwan* has escaped is no longer a contributing member of the household or of village society generally. Failure to perform a ceremony to recall the *khwan* can displease the local spirits, and traditional customary legal practices involving village elders may be invoked to enforce the requirement to pay *kha tham khwan*.

In contemporary Thailand, an individual who no longer lives in a village community is still said to have lost his or her *khwan* when injured. A ceremony to recall the *khwan* may also be required for that person. Because the victim now lives far from the sacred center of his or her birth, however, the collective and locational aspects of the injury have disappeared. The *khwan* may drop from the body at the place where the accident occurred, but that place is not located within a community of humans and spirits, and the *khwan* is no longer described as flying away to the forest near the village. No one views the loss of the *khwan* as a concern to anyone but its owner. As a result of this individuation of injury and of the identity of the injury victim, there is no collective interest in recovering the *khwan*, and there is no set of customary legal practices that can be mobilized to compel the injurer to pay *kha tham khwan*. If the injured person seeks payment for the *khwan*, he or she must find some other mechanism to obtain it.

One may see a similar individuation of injury and identity in the interviewees' description of the "life extension" (*sŭp chata*) ceremony. Many injury victims reported that they performed this ritual—which combines Buddhist and animist elements—to recover spiritually from the effects of the harm and ensure good fortune into the future. Interviewees in this study described the postinjury life extension ceremony as an individualized practice unconnected to any geographically defined community. Yet in rural society, the ceremony can also be a communal event (Damrikun 1999, 281–283) and is locality based because it involves all the households within the village. As one interviewee recalled, the villagewide version of the ceremony connected all the households to one another like a spiritual electric grid:

> We perform the ceremony in the village. They bring incense, candles, and flowers and other things used in offering prayers. They bring everything to the temple, along with sacred string. They bring all the string

that they have and connect it from the temple to the house, just like an electric wire going into the house. They bring the monk's "electrical wire" right into the house. They do this for every household. The monks begin the ceremony in the morning and continue to midnight. They perform the religious ceremony with prayers to expel the ghosts from the house. This is called *süp chata*. They do it once a year. (interview with Bancha)

In the village setting, the collective version of the *süp chata* ritual symbolized the interconnectedness of all households and villagers, the importance to the entire community of each villager's strong and durable personality, and the place-specific conception of community. Interconnectedness was made tangible by the sacred string running from the temple to every house in the village. Yet when the injury victims in our study performed the *süp chata* ceremony to recover from their mishap, the communal version with its geographical specificity was no longer part of their experience. Repair and strengthening of the personality in contemporary Thailand have, as a result of the processes of relocalization and delocalization, been individualized. By performing only the life extension ceremony for a single person, the injury victim symbolically underscores the solitary nature of the quest to improve one's spiritual well-being and prospects in life.

Conclusion

To what extent have the social and economic transformations of the last few decades been accompanied by a change in the relationship between state law and the law of sacred centers? Previously, as we have seen, the two forms of legal mapping interacted in a process of "interlegality." The two types of law were to some extent interdependent. They reinforced and legitimated one another. Although rare, litigation made sense from the perspective of village-level customary law and offered additional assurance that customary remedies would be enforced. State law was an extension of customary law by other means and benefitted the community as a whole.

With globalization, however, the customary law of sacred centers has weakened, and karmic practices and beliefs are now thought to be in conflict with state law. Injured persons often cite their religious beliefs to explain why they have decided not to seek any compensation and why they reject the law. In the past, Buddhism was not necessarily opposed to state law. Indeed, villagers saw Buddhism as consistent with—and to some degree as requiring—the search for compensation, even if that search led injury victims to the Provincial Court. Alongside changes in the concepts of society, self, and responsibility for injury, however, we also see transformations in these interconnections between state law and nonstate law in northern Thailand. Pathways that formerly connected the map of sacred centers to the map of state law have all but disappeared. The pursuit of legal rights and remedies now seems a form of delusion and attachment: a failure to understand the root cause of misfortune and more likely to increase suffering than to end it.

5

Litigation

THE PRECEDING CHAPTERS PORTRAY A BREAKDOWN in village-level customary law associated with Chiangmai's exposure to late-twentieth-century globalization. Because of what we have called the re-localization and delocalization of injuries, ordinary people can no longer depend on the remediation mechanisms that were familiar to their parents and grandparents. Compensation systems linked to sacred centers and village mediators have been weakened and, in many cases, have disappeared completely.

In the past, a small but significant number of injury victims filed lawsuits when their access to customary remedies was blocked. Well-established theories of law and social change would lead us to expect such litigation to have increased in Thailand during the past quarter-century. In his discussion of the theoretical literature on longitudinal court studies, Munger (1990, 220) explains that Hurst (1956; 1964) was among the first to postulate that economic "modernization" brought with it an increased reliance on litigation. Hurst, according to Munger, concluded that "actors facing conflict created by disruption of the social order during economic development turned to law to help them maintain the continuity of that order."[1] Munger observes that Hurst's theory was subsequently modified by Toharia (1976) and by Friedman and Percival (1976), who argued that the relationship between litigation and economic development was not linear but curvilinear: "(L)ong-term trends in litigation were shaped by both the rise in conflict accompanying economic development and the subsequent routinization of social relations following change" (Munger 1990, 221).

According to these theories, Chiangmai's dramatic social and economic changes in the 1980s and 1990s should have been accompanied by pronounced increases in litigation, whether linear or curvilinear. As rural community structures broke down, as individuals migrated to work in unfamiliar settings, as family networks and traditional mediators lost their authority, as new types of interactions and injuries occurred, and as new concepts of rights and rule of law were disseminated by political movements, NGOs, and the media, injured persons should have gone to court to obtain remedies that were no longer available in their new social circumstances.

In this chapter, we begin by asking whether the expected increase in personal injury litigation has in fact occurred. The answer, somewhat surprisingly, appears to be "no." Indeed, there is reason to think that the latest era of global influence has witnessed a decline in the frequency with which injured Chiangmai residents seek legal remedies. In addition to our comparison of personal injury litigation rates from 1965 to 1974 and from 1992 to 1997, we also analyze the content of personal injury case files to determine whether they contain evidence that state law is still connected to customary dispute resolution in a mutually reinforcing relationship, as was apparent in injury cases litigated during the 1960s and 1970s. This comparison of personal injury case records over a thirty-year period will enable us to substantiate our observation in the preceding chapters that the linkages between state and nonstate law have been disrupted and, unexpectedly, personal injury litigation rates have declined.

Formulating Litigation Rates

The term *litigation rate* refers to the frequency with which particular types of cases, such as personal injury claims, are filed as lawsuits.[2] Commentators, however, tend to use the term loosely, and popular references to litigation rates are often misleading. In popular usage, the term seems to mean nothing more than the number of case filings in

PLATE 5.1 *Façade of the Chiangmai Provincial Court, Amphur Muang, Chiangmai. (Patrick Whitaker)*

a given year. If the number increases from one year to the next, commentators and policy makers often claim that citizens have become more "litigious," implying that people are more prone to bring lawsuits in the present than they were in some imagined past. Numerous logical flaws, however, make such assertions essentially meaningless.[3] The first is the problem of the starting point. If comparisons are made to a base year in which the number of filings was particularly low, then a return to the normal number of cases in subsequent years will create the impression that filings have increased, when in fact they have merely reverted to a statistical average. Second, apparent changes in litigation rates from one year to the next may be caused by changes in the law, in the jurisdiction of the courts, or even in clerical practices or the adoption of new record-keeping procedures rather than arising from any change in the attitudes or behavior of the claimants (Saks 1992). Third, the number of case filings may increase or decrease simply because of changes in settlement practices among lawyers or insurers that have nothing to do with the readiness of injured persons to bring claims against their injurers.

A fourth flaw in popular assertions about litigation rates is most relevant to our discussion of personal injury cases in Chiangmai. The concept of a *rate* of litigation implies more than simply the raw number of cases that reach the court. Rather, it is usually assumed to refer to the propensity of individuals who have suffered an injury to bring a lawsuit, and it therefore implies a comparison of the number of lawsuits to the universe of injuries that could have been litigated—Saks (1175) refers to them as "actionable injuries." Logically, a litigation rate should consist of two numbers, a numerator (the number of lawsuits filed in a given year) and a denominator (the number of actionable injuries). Popular discussion of litigation rates, however, usually ignores the concept of the denominator entirely or else makes misleading assumptions about it.

Common sense—and analysis by numerous sociolegal researchers—suggests that the problem of the denominator is crucial. If, as Saks asks us to imagine, the number of lawsuits in a given year increases sharply, we should not conclude that the litigation rate has risen until we have first ruled out the possibility that the number of actionable injuries has also increased. If a rise or fall in the frequency of litigation simply mirrors a rise or fall in the number of actionable injuries, then it would be more accurate to say that litigation rates have remained constant because injured people are no more or less likely to litigate now than they were before. Conversely, an absence of change in the number of lawsuits does not mean that litigation rates have remained stable. If the denominator of actionable injuries but not the number of lawsuits has increased (as we shall see, this appears to have been the case in Chiangmai), then there has actually been a decline in litigiousness although it appears superficially that no change has occurred. In short, without attention to the frequency of actionable injuries, one can say very little about the significance of change—or lack of change—in the number of personal injury lawsuits filed in court.

Although the number of actionable injuries is an essential element in any discussion of litigation rates, it is extremely difficult to ascertain. Reliable statistics about the number of injuries that occur in a given legal jurisdiction are elusive under the best of circumstances; and, even if the number of injuries could somehow be determined, we would still need to know how many of those injuries were "actionable" in the sense that a court would find them to be tortious. Yet, it is impossible to be certain that an injury is actionable without an actual legal determination—that, after all, is the purpose of a trial. Moreover, the process of litigation is itself definitional (see Saks, 1174). Litigation is not simply a clerical process of matching an injury to a fixed set of legal criteria; it is an interpretive and judgmental process that announces from time to time that certain types of injuries are indeed actionable from that point forward.

Because it is all but impossible to determine the true number of actionable injuries in a given year, sociolegal scholars have tended to use population as a second-best substitute. Litigation rates are usually expressed as the number of lawsuits per thousand population. This makes some sense because increases or decreases in the number of lawsuits that simply mirror increases or decreases in the population might seem to represent no change at all in litigation rates. Yet an exclusive reliance on population as the denominator in calculating litigation rates is also deeply flawed. Equating population with the number of actionable injuries assumes that injury rates remain constant within a given population. But is it reasonable to assume, for example, that a community of a million people will always experience ten times as many actionable injuries as a community of 100,000 people? Clearly not. Injury rates may vary within a given population—or differ from one population group to another—depending on many circumstances, such as rapid industrialization, toxic environmental exposures, a proliferation of dangerous consumer products, or an increase in risky technologies or transportation modalities. If the number of lawsuits were to rise markedly under such circumstances while the population remained constant, it would not in any way indicate an increased propensity to sue. Indeed, the *rate* of litigation per actionable injury might in this situation remain unchanged despite a dramatic rise in the number of lawsuits per thousand population, as long as the increase in lawsuits remained proportional to the increase in harms suffered. Thus, population alone is an unsatisfactory solution to the problem of ascertaining the denominator when constructing litigation rates; but, as we shall see, it is often difficult to find a better one.

Have Personal Injury Litigation Rates in Chiangmai Declined?

Although prevailing theories of law and social change would predict a substantial increase in personal injury litigation rates during the period of rapid socioeconomic change Chiangmai experienced over the past quarter-century, the best indicators suggest—surprisingly—that the opposite has occurred, and personal injury litigation rates have actually declined. To support this conclusion, we must analyze changes in both the numerator (number of personal injury lawsuits filed) and the denominator (number of actionable injuries) over the period for which statistics are available: 1965 to 1997.

Figure 5.1 presents the "numerator"—the raw number of tort cases filed in the Chiangmai Provincial Court during the two periods we researched, 1965 to 1974 and 1992 to 1997. In the earlier period, we compiled statistics at three-year intervals, but in the later period we compiled them every year. Moreover, in the later period we were able to break down tort litigation into personal injury and property damage cases, but in the earlier period we were not able to distinguish the two types of tort cases.

As we have seen, litigation figures of this kind are usually presented in relation to population. Because Chiangmai's population grew

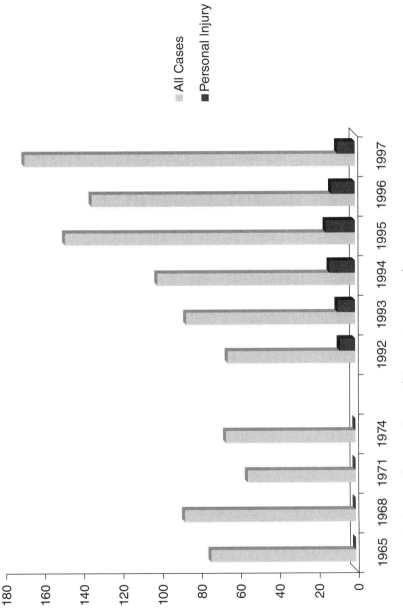

FIGURE 5.1 *Tort Cases in Chiangmai Provincial Court, 1965 to 1974 and 1992 to 1997.*

TABLE 5.1

Tort Litigation Rates per Population in Chiangmai, Thailand (1965 to 1997)

Year	Population Served by Court[1]	Tort Cases	Personal Injury Cases[2]	Tort Cases per 1,000 Pop.
1965	909,958	74	—	0.081
1968	968,738	87	—	0.090
1971	1,023,223	55	—	0.054
1974	1,086,203	66	—	0.061
1992	1,307,698	65	8	0.050
1993	1,313,735	86	9	0.066
1994	1,325,656	101	13	0.076
1995	1,332,060	148	15	0.111
1996	1,343,927	134	12	0.100
1997	1,352,984	169	9	0.125

[1]Population figures are from National Statistical Office of Thailand 1966–1998. "Population Served by Court" is less than the total population of Chiangmai Province for 1992–1997. During this later period, a separate trial court in Fang District served three of Chingmai's twenty-four districts (Fang, Mae Ai, and Chai Prakan), whose populations have therefore been subtracted from the total for the province.

[2]Data available from 1965 to 1974 do not permit a breakdown of tort cases by personal injury and non-personal-injury claims.

substantially from 1965 to 1997, Table 5.1 displays changes in "litigation rates" in which the rise in population is considered in relation to the increased number of tort cases filed in the Chiangmai Provincial Court.

Several aspects of Table 5.1 are of particular interest. It is obvious that the rate of tort litigation per 1,000 population was relatively low to begin with and has remained quite low over a period of more than three decades. The mean rate in the earlier period (1965 to 1974) was 0.071 cases per thousand population, and the mean rate in the later period (1992 to 1997) increased very slightly to 0.088 cases per thousand population. By comparison, the tort litigation rate in our home state of New York in 2000 was 4.127 cases per thousand population—almost 47 times greater than the more recent mean rate in Chiangmai.[4] In 2000, the tort litigation rate in Michigan was 2.238 cases per thousand population, and in Ohio it was 2.660 tort cases per thousand population[5]—tort litigation rates that exceeded Chiangmai's mean rate from 1992 to 1997 by factors of more than twenty-five and thirty, respectively. Even if the comparison is to an American state whose rural population more nearly approaches Chiangmai's figure of 73.5 percent, the American rate is still substantially higher. Maine is the most predominantly rural American state for which complete tort data are available, and its litigation rate in 2000 was 0.983 cases per thousand population—a low figure but still more than eleven times greater than Chiangmai's mean rate from 1992 to 1997.[6] The next most rural American state for which complete data are available is Arkansas, with a tort litigation rate of 1.646 cases per thousand—almost nineteen times the mean rate in Chiangmai from 1992 to 1997.[7]

It is difficult to find comparable data in other societies. Ietswaart (1990, 583) reports the results of rather limited studies in selected jurisdictions of several European countries in the early 1980s. The tort litigation rates sampled in those countries include the Netherlands (0.1 tort cases per thousand in 1982), France (0.3 tort cases per thousand in 1984), and Belgium (5.0 tort cases per thousand in 1984). Thus, the Netherlands tort litigation rate in 1982 was approximately equal to the highest rates recorded in Chiangmai in the 1990s. The French rate in 1984 was more than three times Chiangmai's mean rate from 1992 to 1997, and the Belgian rate in 1984 was almost fifty-seven times Chiangmai's mean rate from 1992 to 1997. All of these comparisons to the United States and Europe are very crude because they do not take account of differences in court structure, criteria of liability, procedural differences, settlement practices, court and lawyers' fees (particularly the contingent fee permitted in the United States but prohibited in Europe and Thailand), and many other important factors that might affect the frequency of filings apart from—or in relation to—the propensity to sue. Nevertheless, they provide a rough indication that Chiangmai's tort litigation rates are relatively low by any standard.

Although tort litigation rates per population in Chiangmai increased very little from the earlier period of 1965 to 1974 to the later period of 1992 to 1997, in the three most recent years (1995, 1996, and 1997), the rate rose to a slightly higher level of 0.111, 0.100, and 0.125 cases per thousand population, respectively. Do these figures suggest an upward trend, albeit a modest one? Here the ability to differentiate personal injury cases from other torts is useful. Although the number of tort cases as a whole increased from 1992 to 1997, the number of *personal injury* cases did not. As Figure 5.2 illustrates, the change in the number of litigated tort cases overall was attributable to a slight rise in property damage claims.

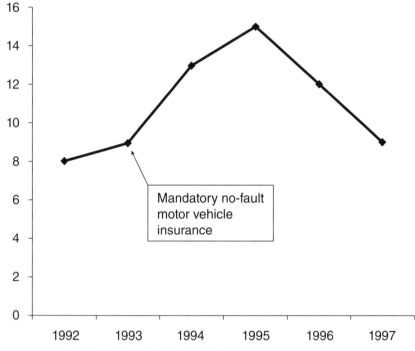

FIGURE 5.2 *Personal Injury Tort Cases Litigated, 1992 to 1997.*

When tort litigation rates are analyzed over time in relation to Chiangmai's population, the results suggest that there has been little change from 1965 to 1997. Litigation rates started relatively low and remained about the same, even as the society of northern Thailand experienced very dramatic transformations. Yet, as we have seen, calculating litigation rates in terms of population is problematic. If we wish to determine whether social change has been associated with a change in legal consciousness and in particular an increased propensity to sue, it would be much better to compare the number of tort filings to the number of actionable injuries that occurred in Chiangmai each year.

Unfortunately, but not surprisingly, there are no credible records of the number of injuries—much less the number of actionable injuries—that occurred in Chiangmai from 1965 to 1997.[8] Nevertheless, there is good reason to think that such injuries have increased greatly. The use of population as a proxy for the number of actionable injuries in Chiangmai most likely understates by a very substantial amount the extent to which personal injuries have increased. If this is the case, then what appears to be no significant change in the tort litigation rates over time is actually a substantial decrease.

Why do we suspect that the number of actionable injuries in Chiangmai has increased much more rapidly than the population has grown? Simply because most injuries are associated with highway accidents. This was certainly true in our pool of potential interviewees in a large Chiangmai hospital. Our interview sample of thirty-five subjects was selected from a group of ninety-three individuals treated at a major Chiangmai hospital for accidental injuries over a five-month period. This larger group consisted of every injured patient who expressed a willingness to be interviewed and, because almost no one declined to take part in the study, was reasonably representative of all injured persons admitted to the hospital. Out of these ninety-three patients, seventy (75.3 percent) were injured in highway accidents, which leads us to conclude that cars and motorcycles are associated with a significant portion of all accidental injuries in Chiangmai—including those that might be actionable.

Assuming that highway accidents constitute the bulk of actionable injuries, then a sharp increase in such accidents should have brought a corresponding increase in tort cases. There is no question that personal injury litigation in Chiangmai was closely connected to highway accidents. In fact, of the sixty-six personal injury claims litigated in the Chiangmai Provincial Court from 1992 to 1997, sixty-three (95 percent) grew out of traffic accidents. Tort litigation does mirror injuries in the broader society in the sense that cars and motorcycles are associated with a large percentage of cases both in the hospital and in the courthouse. Nevertheless, the filing of personal injury claims appears to have lagged far behind the growing rate of actionable injuries that must have arisen from increased highway accidents.

Although there are no reliable direct statistics on highway injuries in Chiangmai from the 1960s to the present, there are statistics that can plausibly serve as an indirect measure. It is reasonable to assume that the more motor vehicles there are on the highway, the greater the number of accidents and injuries that will occur. We cannot count the injuries, but we can count the motor vehicles because registration is compulsory, and credible data on vehicle registration have been reported each year from 1965 to 1997.[9] While not perfect, these figures are at least relatively accurate. Drivers of unregistered vehicles would be subject to fine and punishment, and personal observation confirms that most cars, motorcycles, trucks, and buses do in fact have licenses and were therefore registered and counted in the official statistics. Figure 5.3 displays the data gleaned from these annual reports.

If vehicle registration statistics can serve as a reliable proxy for the frequency of actionable injuries in Chiangmai, then it is reasonable to infer that the dramatic increase in motor vehicles was accompanied by a corresponding increase in injuries that could be litigated. Between 1965 and 1997, the number of registered vehicles in Chiangmai province increased by a factor of 79.2 (from 8,547 to 677,123), but the number of tort cases from 1965 to 1997 increased by a factor of merely 2.3 (from seventy-four to 169). The increase in the number of motor vehicles (our proxy for personal injuries) was, in other words, more than 34.4 times greater than the increase in tort cases.

If actionable injuries have indeed increased dramatically while tort litigation (even unadjusted for population) has experienced extremely modest growth at best, then we can only conclude that the percentage of actionable injuries that become lawsuits has *decreased* significantly. In short, there is compelling evidence to suggest that the tort litigation rate in Chiangmai has dropped substantially from 1965 to 1997, contrary to all expectations that globalization would be accompanied by exactly the opposite result. It is remarkable that, during the six-year period 1992 to 1997, as the number of motorcycles and cars on the roadways skyrocketed, only sixty-six personal injury cases were litigated—*an average of only eleven personal injury cases per year out of a population of more than 1.3 million people!*

Additional confirmation of a decrease in personal injury litigation comes from an unexpected source. As discussed in Chapter 3, individuals who suffer personal injuries in Thailand may choose to litigate their claims as criminal cases; and, because the purpose of private criminal

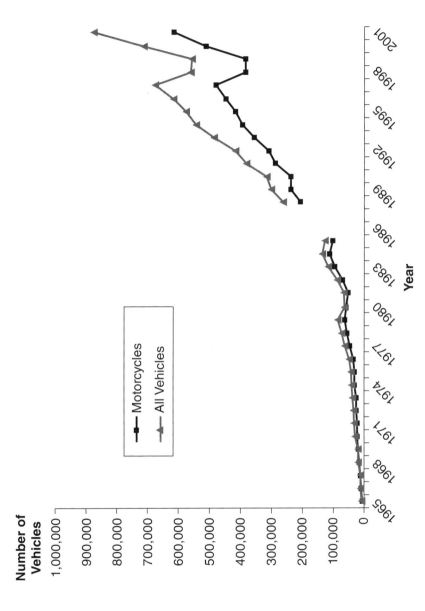

FIGURE 5.3 *Vehicle Registration in Chiangmai, 1965 to 2002.*

litigation in actuality is to stimulate out-of-court settlements, they are similar in their remedial function to tort actions. It is significant, therefore, that private criminal litigation of injury cases has also declined substantially over the past quarter-century. During the *four years* of our earlier study (1965, 1968, 1971, and 1974), injury victims brought thirty-three private criminal actions;[10] but, during the *six years* from 1992 to 1997, they litigated only eight private criminal cases in the Chiangmai Provincial Court. The decline in injury-related private criminal cases from a yearly average of 8.25 cases to a yearly average of 1.33 cases parallels the apparent decline in injury-related tort litigation in Chiangmai from 1965 to 1997 and indirectly confirms the general trend away from the formal invocation of law.

Legal Consciousness and the Apparent Decline in Personal Injury Litigation Rates

We cannot say exactly why injury litigation rates appear to have dropped sharply from the earlier period to the present, but it is reasonable to assume that a change in legal consciousness played a part and that the relationship between legal consciousness and litigation behavior is mutually reinforcing. As we have seen in the preceding chapters, interviews with injured people provide strong indications of a shift in legal consciousness. That is, ordinary people in Thailand think about law and legal institutions in different ways at the turn of the twenty-first century as compared to the 1960s and 1970s. It is not necessary to claim that this shift in legal consciousness alone *caused* injury litigation rates to drop; it is enough to note that changes in legal consciousness and litigation rates in this instance went hand in hand. Transformations in the way they think about law and legal institutions make injured persons in contemporary Thailand more averse to litigation, while at the same time the infrequency and relative invisibility of personal injury lawsuits affect popular consciousness of law and make it less likely that ordinary people will even contemplate the option of litigation when they suffer potentially actionable injuries. The mutually constitutive relationship between legal consciousness and the use or nonuse of formal legal institutions has been the subject of considerable scholarly attention (e.g., Sarat and Kearns 1995; Ewick and Silbey 1998; Engel and Munger, 2003).

Although our primary point is to underscore the mutually reinforcing quality of changes in legal consciousness and litigation rates, it is also important to note that other factors could play a causal role in the decreased willingness to invoke the law in injury cases. In this section, we identify some of these factors and discuss the likelihood that they have affected the downward trend in injury litigation from the earlier period, 1965 to 1974, to the later period, 1992 to 1997. As a preliminary matter, we should mention that we asked insurance adjusters, personal injury lawyers, judges, and legal scholars to help us identify other factors that might account for the apparent decline in tort litigation rates. No one could point to anything other than a shift in the consciousness of injured persons. No significant change in tort law or procedure occurred between the two periods of our research, 1965 to 1974 and 1992 to 1997. No restructuring of the courts had taken place between those two periods that might have restricted access to injury claimants, nor were there new cost factors that made tort litigation more expensive than it was in the past. In the absence of any obvious legal or structural changes, therefore, we have attempted to identify other less obvious factors that may have contributed to the apparent decrease in the resort to law in injury cases.

Changes in Customary Settlement Practices

It appears that there has been a decline in the customary law settlement of injury claims mediated by village chiefs and others. In some societies, such a decline might be expected to produce an increase in the litigation of those unresolved claims. In northern Thailand, however, we suspect that the result could have been precisely the opposite: Injury litigation rates may actually have *decreased* because of the decline in customary nonjudicial settlement practices. We searched the sixty-six tort cases filed from 1992 to 1997 for evidence of prior settlement negotiations to determine whether the Chiangmai Provincial Court is still being used as an enforcement mechanism—a court of last resort— for customary law. Such evidence had been abundant in our previous study of the case files of injury lawsuits filed from 1965 to 1974 (Engel 1978, 133–152). In our more recent data, however, we found mention of nonjudicial settlement activity in only sixteen of the sixty-six cases filed from 1992 to 1997—approximately 2.7 tort cases per year. Significantly, none of these sixteen cases involved village chiefs or other respected elders serving as mediators. The nonjudicial negotiations mentioned in all of them took place at the police station. Police mediators, unlike village chiefs, are not spokespersons for customary law. They speak the language of traffic regulations and not local spirits or Buddhism. In short, there is no evidence in any of the personal injury cases litigated from 1992 to 1997 that the Chiangmai Provincial Court is still used to enforce and legitimate customary legal practices, and its failure to perform this role may help to explain the decline in its use.

Antipathy toward Government Officials and Legal Institutions

It is tempting to theorize that use of the law in injury cases has declined because ordinary Thai people fear or distrust the official legal system and are reluctant to go to court when they suffer injuries. The interviewees did at times speak of their apprehensions about dealing with Thai officialdom. They feared that resort to litigation might expose them to unfair treatment and even retaliation by powerful adversaries and corrupt officials. Is it possible that the decline in injury litigation and embrace of Buddhist values of forgiveness, compassion, and generosity might be simply an expression of this fear, which is the deeper cause of the recent changes we have observed? We think the answer is no.

Our three decades of longitudinal data provide unique advantages in addressing this question. Viewing tort litigation over this long span of time, we are able to suggest with some confidence that the legal consciousness of injury victims underwent a significant transformation during a period in which there was no apparent increase in popular antipathy toward government officials and institutions. While tort litigation rates declined and new forms of religiosity led injury victims to reject liberal legalism more decisively than ever before, the popular distrust of Thai government officials and legal institutions remained about the same. If anything, citizens' attitudes toward Thai officialdom in the late 1990s were more positive than during the 1960s and 1970s, which was an era of repressive military dictatorships marked by occasional bloody violence toward prodemocracy activists. We asked all of our interviewees to describe their recent interactions with a number of Thai government institutions, including the police, district offices, provincial offices, and the courts. To be sure, they expressed wariness about such contacts, but this wariness did not appear to have increased over time in a way that might explain a diminished use of the courts or the law. Our interviewees told us that they thought matters had actually improved quite a bit in recent years and that official institutions today, although still intimidating, were more responsive to the public—and to them personally—than in the past. These views were consistent with the advent of democratic elections and the passage of a "People's Constitution" in 1997.

Thus, while there was an apparent shift away from Thai tort law from the 1960s to the 1990s, there was no corresponding increase in popular fears of government institutions and officials. It does not make sense, therefore, to conclude that fear of Thai officialdom was the primary cause of the decline in law and legal consciousness that we have documented. The explanation for this decline cannot rest on a heightened antipathy toward government officials and legal institutions and probably lies elsewhere.

Changes in Liability Insurance Practices

Between the two periods in which we surveyed tort litigation rates, insurance was required for all who drive registered motor vehicles (Royal Edict Concerning Persons Injured by Vehicles, 1992). During our earlier research from 1965 to 1974, motor vehicle liability insurance was voluntary and, at least in Chiangmai, was rare; but the legislation made it mandatory throughout Thailand starting in 1993. The impact of insurance on the litigation of personal injury cases is difficult to determine, and researchers have not, to our knowledge, asked whether developments in Thai insurance coverage have tended to increase, decrease, or have no significant effect on litigation rates. Certainly, routine nonjudicial settlements with insurance companies under a modified no-fault arrangement are now possible, yet the interviews with individual injury victims suggest that such settlements are small and often unsatisfactory if they occur at all. The maximum coverage for personal injury under the mandatory basic plan is only 10,000 *baht* (approximately $250), and most of the serious injury cases we studied involved losses much greater than that amount. As we shall see in the next section, the mean amount of the damage awards in successful tort cases from 1992 to 1997 was 189,152 *baht*—nearly nineteen times the maximum coverage under the basic plan. In any event, liability insurance payments were not a prominent feature of the injury narratives, and, in fact, interviewees usually did not mention them. It appears significant that the number of personal injury cases litigated in Chiangmai after the mandatory motor vehicle insurance law took effect in 1993 actually increased for three years and never fell lower than the number of cases litigated in 1992 (see Figure 5.2 above). Passage of the law did not seem to reduce personal injury cases in Chiangmai.

One insurance agent explained that insurance had little effect on the attitudes and practices of injury victims because they considered the small payments to be insignificant and irrelevant. The central issue, she contended, is the personal relationship between the injured person and the injurer: "Most people want the other party to pay *something*. They're not satisfied if they get paid only by the insurance company." Under current law, moreover, injured persons can still bring lawsuits against defendants or their insurance companies for damages that exceed the basic coverage plan, and six of the sixty-six injury cases litigated from 1992 to 1997 named insurance companies as convenient deep-pocket defendants. Furthermore, plaintiffs' insurance companies can sue defendants by exercising their right of subrogation: Ten of the sixty-six injury cases fit this description. Thus, motor vehicle insurance is now part of the litigation picture in Chiangmai, but there is no evidence thus far that it has diminished the rate of tort litigation.

Changes in Social Insurance

Some changes in Thai social health insurance occurred between 1965 to 1974 and 1992 to 1997, and we should consider whether these changes might have decreased the necessity for injured persons to seek compensation from their injurers by tort litigation or other means.[11] We are not aware of any research that examines the connections between evolving Thai social health insurance schemes, both voluntary and mandatory, and the use or nonuse of tort law, but we think it unlikely that there was a substantial connection during the time period in question. That is because relatively few people in Chiangmai were covered by social insurance plans at that time, and the compensation of those who were covered was too modest to prevent them from seeking additional compensation from the injurer.[12] Among the changes in social insurance that took place within the period of time between 1965 to 1974 and 1992 to 1997, five deserve mention.

The Workers Compensation Scheme of 1974. This scheme covered work-related illnesses, injuries, death, and disability for employees in firms with more than ten workers. Employment-related coverage under this plan probably had a limited impact, if any, on the consciousness or law-related behavior of injury victims. Charoenloet (1997, 24) observes that by the mid-1990s only some 100 work-related cases per year were compensated by the workers' compensation fund *in the entire country of Thailand.* We analyzed the screening information obtained from our original sample of all ninety-three accident victims admitted to the hospital (from whom we selected our thirty-five interviewees) to determine how many of them were likely to have held work-related health coverage. We concluded that two-thirds (sixty-two persons) of the injury victims admitted to the hospital probably were not even covered by workers' compensation—because they were not employed in a firm with over ten workers or because they worked part-time, were self-employed, or were unemployed.[13]

The Low-Income Medical Welfare Scheme of 1975. This plan used tax revenues to pay medical costs incurred by the poor and in 1992 was "extended to cover other groups, such as the elderly, children younger than 12 years old and disabled people" (Tangcharoensathien, Wibulpholprasert, and Nitayaramphong 2004b, 751). Even the limited benefits provided by this scheme failed in many instances to reach the intended beneficiaries. According to Tangcharoensathien et al. (2004a,

179), a Thai Ministry of Public Health survey in 1996 had found that 28 percent of the poorest households in the country, which should have been covered under this plan, were actually uninsured because of "seasonal variation and difficulty of income assessment" (Id., 184). Because of this plan's shortcomings and limitations, it is unlikely that it played more than a minor role in the transformation of legal consciousness and litigation patterns between 1965 to 1974 and 1992 to 1997.

The Civil Servant Medical Benefit Scheme of 1980. This plan benefited only government employees and their dependents, a group representing roughly 10 percent of Thailand's population as of 1996 (Tangcharoensathien, Supachutikul, and Lertiendumrong 1999, 914). Because the group covered is a relatively small portion of the total population, and because the plan covers only medical costs, it probably had a limited effect if any on the legal consciousness or litigation practices of injured people throughout Chiangmai.

The Government Health Card Program, Initiated in 1983. This was a voluntary plan aimed at rural residents who wished to—and could afford to—pay half of its annual cost of 1,000 *baht* per household (the other half was subsidized by the Ministry of Public Health) (Supakankunti 2000, 86). Like the others, this plan probably had a limited impact, at best, on the compensation of the varied and extensive costs associated with serious injuries. Participants in the plan were self-selected, and observers noted that those who opted into the program were often those who were already ill—not those who were healthy but might subsequently suffer an accidental injury. As one study of the Health Card Program concluded, "The sick usually joined while the healthy opted out.... [I]t did not protect against catastrophic expenses" (World Health Organization [WHO] 2003, 6).

The Social Security Scheme, Enacted in 1990. This plan initially extended coverage to include non-work-related illnesses and injuries for workers employed by firms with more than twenty employees, but by 1994 it was expanded to include workers in firms with more than ten employees. Persons employed by such firms constituted 7.3 percent of Thailand's population in 1995 (Supakankunti, 87; see generally Tangcharoensathien et al. 2004a, 176–178). This figure is probably higher in Bangkok and lower elsewhere in Thailand (including Chiangmai), although precise breakdowns are not available (Mills et al. 2000, 166). As noted in our analysis of the pool of potential interviewees who had been admitted to the hospital for treatment of injuries, there is reason to think that the number of injured persons in Chiangmai who worked for firms of this size and could avail themselves of this form of medical assistance was relatively small.

•   •   •

To summarize, although the provision of social health insurance in Thailand did change in many ways between 1965 to 1974 and 1992 to 1997, it seems unlikely that any of these changes had more than a modest impact on the legal consciousness of injury victims or significantly diminished the likelihood that they would bring a lawsuit. In particular, the available evidence provides little support for the proposition that ordinary people during this period increasingly avoided the legal system because of new forms of compensation they received through these government-sponsored plans. Tangcharoensathien et al. (2004a, 179) note that in 1991 only a third of Thailand's population had *any* form of public or private health insurance, a number that increased nationwide to the still-low figure of 46 percent by 1996 near the end of the period covered by our second docket survey. Moreover, even individuals who did acquire new forms of coverage during that period could have used tort law to recover losses that social insurance did not cover, such as damages based on pain and suffering, lost wages both past and future, and funeral expenses (Thai Civil and Commercial Code 1935, §§446, 444, and 443). For these reasons, we must tentatively reject the possibility that the decline in tort law between 1965 to 1974 and 1992 to 1997 was caused by the introduction of new forms of social insurance.

The Bar and the Supply of Lawyers

The number of lawyers available to represent injury victims might also affect litigation rates. Had there been a reduction in the supply of lawyers in Chiangmai since 1965, it might have contributed to the apparent decrease in tort litigation in the Chiangmai Provincial Court. Although we could not obtain documentary evidence on the Chiangmai bar for 1965, officials at the Thai Law Society estimated that the number of lawyers in Chiangmai at that time did not exceed 100. By contrast, the number of registered attorneys in Chiangmai in 2001–2002 totaled 577.[14] Most Chiangmai attorneys operate out of small offices with one or two partners at most, and they handle a broad range of cases—including personal injuries. Thus, the supply of lawyers who might litigate tort cases did not decrease from 1965 to 1997. On the contrary, the number of attorneys during that time span probably increased more than five-fold.[15] If anything, the growth of the Chiangmai bar would lead us to expect an increase in the rate of tort litigation rather than the decrease that apparently occurred.

In conclusion, in this section we have considered five factors that might have contributed to the transformations in legal consciousness and litigation behavior that occurred in Chiangmai between 1965 to 1974 and 1992 to 1997. Because much of the injury pyramid in Thailand is still uncharted territory, we cannot definitively rule out some of these causal factors. Yet the evidence now available leads us to think that there is no obvious factor in the middle levels of the pyramid that can explain the drop-off in formal legal activity that has occurred at the top of the pyramid—other than the growing ineffectiveness of customary law. We are not ready to assert that the decline of customary law and the corresponding shift in legal consciousness at the base of the pyramid are the only causes of the diminished flow of cases into the Chiangmai Provincial Court, although that possibility must be considered. It is safe to say, however, that trends at the highest and lowest levels of the injury pyramid have moved in the same direction—away from formal legal recourse—and were almost certainly mutually reinforcing.

The Content of Personal Injury Cases

We turn now from the apparent decline in personal injury litigation rates to the relatively few injury cases that did make their way to the Chiangmai Provincial Court. We ask what the characteristics of these cases were, how they were resolved, and what light they shed on the disconnection between customary and state law.

For the most part, personal injury lawsuits were bland and routinized requests for compensation, generally arising out of traffic-related injuries. The plaintiffs usually received some compensation as a result of their efforts. Defendants won outright victories in only six of the sixty-six personal injury cases (9.5 percent of the total). In nineteen cases (28.8 percent), plaintiffs received favorable verdicts after trial in amounts ranging from 60,116 *baht* to 651,440 *baht*, with a mean award of 189,152 *baht*. In twenty-eight cases (42.4 percent), plaintiffs and defendants reached court-approved settlements in amounts ranging from 10,000 *baht* to 750,000 *baht*. The mean amount of in-court settlements was 100,000 *baht*. Plaintiffs withdrew nine cases without disclosing terms of the settlement, if any, and three cases were still pending at the time the docket study was completed. In short, personal injury litigation was essentially an unremarkable bureaucratic procedure by means of which most plaintiffs were able to obtain substantial compensation, either through a formal verdict or a court-supervised settlement.

As we have seen, insurance companies now play a part in personal injury litigation, appearing both as plaintiffs (ten of the sixty-six injury cases) and as defendants (six cases). We were told by an insurance adjuster that most injury victims were not satisfied to receive payment only from the injurer's insurance company, and several of the cases bear out this anecdotal observation. In a 1997 case involving two men named Kham Phongjina and Sombun Metprasopsan, for example, the terms of the court-approved settlement specified that the defendant's insurance company would pay 150,000 *baht*, while the defendant himself was required to pay an additional 50,000 *baht*. The observation that injury victims in Chiangmai expect an injurer to pay something out of his or her own pocket is consistent with descriptions of injury settlement practices in Japan (Tanase 1990), where payouts by insurance companies are seen as insufficient to satisfy the moral obligations injurers personally owe their victims. In America, by contrast, an injury victim's attempt to obtain "blood money" from the injurer's own assets in excess of his or her insurance coverage may be viewed as inappropriate and even immoral (Baker 2001).

In general, however, these sixty-six tort cases lack the rich and colorful detail that could be found in the case files of the 1960s and 1970s. Personal injury litigation, besides being extremely rare, has become formalistic and routinized. Only two or three cases provide glimpses into the surrounding culture and the systems of customary law that traditionally dealt with injury cases. One such case brought by Phra Ratrattanakon and Phrakhru Phiphatrattanaphong against Thawonwong, Ltd., in 1995 involved two Buddhist monks who were hit by a speeding truck while standing by the side of a highway after their vehicle suffered a minor accident. The driver of the truck immediately fled the scene of the accident without offering aid or assistance. The plaintiff and defendant later negotiated an informal settlement for 300,000 *baht* at a police station near the scene of the accident. It is not surprising that the defendant was willing to settle this case nonjudicially. Few people could be expected to sympathize with the employer of a hit-and-run driver who had seriously injured two members of the clergy. When the defendant failed to comply with the terms of the nonjudicial settlement agreement, however, the two plaintiffs (represented by a lay spokesperson) brought a tort action in the Chiangmai Provincial Court nine months later. Perhaps the defendant had thought it could escape its obligation to pay the injured monks because its place of business was located in the distant province of Saraburi, near Bangkok. In any event, the Chiangmai Provincial Court decided the case with remarkable speed, awarding the full amount of 300,000 *baht* to the monks just twelve days after they filed their claim.

The lawsuit brought by the two injured monks, cryptic though it is in certain respects, does provide indications of the cultural factors that influenced the behavior of the parties and ultimately led the plaintiffs to use the court. Moreover, this case demonstrates how the court, through its extraordinarily speedy resolution of the lawsuit in just twelve days, reinforced cultural norms of respect for the clergy and support for agreements mediated by the police. In short, the case resembles litigation from the 1960s and 1970s, in which it was clear that state law was closely connected to nonstate practices and supportive of them. Cases of this kind are, however, extremely rare. Only a few of them provide the same sort of window into local cultural norms and practices that was far more common in the lawsuits brought to the Chiangmai Provincial Court a quarter of a century earlier.

Furthermore, the complex and multilayered causal explanations that are typically offered by injury victims in everyday discourse were conspicuously absent in the litigation files. In their simplified and legalistic treatment of causation, the cases litigated in the Chiangmai Provincial Court further distance themselves from the cultural setting in which they arose. As described in earlier chapters, the nonjudicial narratives of injured persons nearly always presented the causation of their mishap as complex and multiply determined. Injuries never resulted from a single cause, such as the defendant's negligence. They always occurred because of the convergence of negligence with several other factors such as the victim's karma, her fate, her stars, and the intervention of ghosts. None of these other causal factors, however, plays any overt role in the injury cases that are now presented to the Chiangmai court for resolution. Their absence underscores the disconnection between personal injury litigation and the broader cultural context.

For example, in a 1993 case brought by Ms. Rampha Sekajan against Mr. Sakda Inthakaew arising out of a highway accident, the pleadings referred to only one cause of plaintiff's injuries: the defendant's negligence. According to the pleadings, the defendant drove a large ten-wheel truck full of rocks for road construction work. The plaintiff rode in the passenger seat of a pickup truck driven by her husband. Her vehicle came to a stop at an intersection and then proceeded to cross the highway. Other oncoming traffic slowed to let them across, but, the plaintiff contended, the defendant drove carelessly without taking the precautions that a reasonable person in his situation would observe. He drove at a high speed, passing other vehicles that had slowed down. When the defendant got to the intersection, plaintiff's truck was halfway across the road, but defendant was unable to stop his large vehicle in time, "which was the *cause* of the death of Mr. Warakan Sekajan and the bodily injuries received by the plaintiff" (emphasis added).

In her complaint, Ms. Rampha never mentions karma, spirits, fate, or her stars. She cites only the defendant's negligence, and even that reference is made in the most cursory fashion. When she appeared in court,

her testimony, as transcribed in the court records, was equally laconic on
the topic of causation:

> As our car began to turn right onto the highway, the ten-wheel truck
> driven by the defendant came from the direction of the airport, passing
> other vehicles that had slowed to make way for us. He struck the truck
> driven by my husband near the driver's side door. I was knocked uncon-
> scious. The defendant's ten-wheel truck was speeding, and the driver was
> not being careful.

When injury cases enter the rarified atmosphere of the court, causal
explanations that are extremely important to the parties in everyday life
tend to drop out of the discussion. The judges and attorneys would have
found it highly unusual and inappropriate if Ms. Rampha had described
the cause of her accident in the same terms she would undoubtedly use
when talking about it in most other social settings. It is intriguing to
note, however, that Ms. Rampha's courtroom testimony does mention a
detail omitted by her lawyer in the formal complaint. She states that she
later returned to the scene of the accident and saw that the defendant's
truck had dragged her vehicle off the road about thirty meters and had
collided with two motorcycles, a telephone relay box, the bathroom of a
nearby house, and a tamarind tree.

This last detail is intriguing. As we have seen, many injured persons
who participated in the hospital interviews explained the cause of their
misfortune in terms of ghosts near the highway. They told us that ghosts
typically dwell in identifiable trees near the accident site. The plaintiff's
mention of a tamarind tree in the path of defendant's truck raises the possibility that she believes the tree to be inhabited by ghosts who obscured
the defendant's vision or caused him to lose control of his truck. If that
was her real belief, however, she scrupulously avoided saying so when she
testified. Ms. Rampha, like the legal professionals with whom she dealt,
recognized that legal narratives must be constructed on entirely different premises. As Rosen (2006, 68) observes, "Legal systems create facts
in order to treat them as facts. . . . (S)omething must first be regarded as
a fact if it is to count as such." Ghosts, spirits, and even karma are not
"facts" in the context of Thai tort law, despite their importance in Thai
society. The discourse of injury victims in the courthouse is divorced

from the culture in which the accidents occurred, just as litigation is now essentially cut off from customary beliefs and remediation systems.

Conclusion

While litigation may provide compensation that injury victims are otherwise unable to receive, it does so on its own terms. Litigation has become a rarely invoked remediation procedure that operates autonomously in Thai culture. It no longer vindicates or legitimates customary law or gives meaning to the cultural beliefs and expectations of ordinary people in Thailand.

The content of contemporary injury case files points in the same direction as their declining frequency over the past quarter-century. The pleadings and the witness testimony in cases brought before the Chiangmai Provincial Court suggest that the interconnections between law and customary practice have atrophied. It is no longer accurate to say that litigation represents an acceptable final stage in the customary procedures for resolving injury cases, nor does state law reinforce customary practices in any significant way.

As we have seen, the rate of tort litigation has probably diminished substantially in relation to the number of actionable injuries in Chiangmai. This likely decline in the use of law parallels a shift in the consciousness of injured persons that was evident in the interviews with hospital patients and others. Injured persons now view law as even less relevant than in the 1960s and 1970s—a shift in consciousness that runs contrary to the usual expectations of sociolegal theorists. We view these apparent transformations at the top and bottom of the injury pyramid as mutually reinforcing. Although more research is needed to understand possible changes in the middle regions of the Thai tort pyramid, the findings from our study substantiate a fundamental point: The law has become more remote than ever from the lives of ordinary people, and when they suffer injuries they are more likely to turn to other ways of interpreting and responding to their experiences. As the consciousness of injury victims shifts toward nonlegal interpretive frameworks, litigation becomes less attractive to them as a potential course of action; and as tort litigation in Chiangmai becomes extremely rare, it is even less likely that injured persons will have any awareness of the possibility that they could use the law.

Our prior research in Thailand during the 1960s and 1970s, before the accelerated impact of global influences, suggested that state law and customary law interconnected and, at least to some extent, mutually reinforced one another. Our research in the 1990s, however, suggests that these interconnections have all but disappeared, and law now stands isolated from the social and cultural milieu in which ordinary Thai people live. If the pathway between law and custom has indeed been lost in injury cases, we must ask what the concept of justice now means to ordinary people and how they believe it can be attained. That is the subject of the next chapter.

6

Justice

FOR MOST INJURY VICTIMS AND POTENTIAL LITIGANTS in Chiangmai, the pathway between familiar customary remedial practices and official law has been lost. Interconnections that were once tenuous but sometimes significant have now been almost completely obliterated. Injury victims almost never frame their narratives in terms of law, nor does law even enter their consciousness as they consider what has happened to them and what they might do about it. Personal injury cases have nearly disappeared from the docket of the Chiangmai Provincial Court.

Injury victims in contemporary Chiangmai find themselves in an anomalous position: The role of state law has diminished, but so has the role of customary law. Those who suffer injuries feel that they have no place to turn, and most of them express the view that an aggressive demand for compensation would violate fundamental religious precepts and lead in the long run to greater suffering. If that is the case, then it is worth asking what the concept of "justice" has come to mean and how it is that ordinary Thais think justice can be achieved nowadays, if at all. To what extent is law an instrument of justice, and to what extent is justice to be found outside the legal system?

To address these questions, we must first confront some difficult issues of translation. The words *law* and *justice* have specific meanings in English for which the Thai language has no exact equivalents. To discuss these issues with our interviewees, we had to find a way to couch our questions in a vocabulary that was both understandable and meaningful to them. *Law* is usually translated as *kotmai*, which literally means "rule" or "regulation" (Haas 1964, 2). *Kotmai* is somewhat narrower than *law*. Although the term was readily understandable to our interviewees, when they were asked about *kotmai* they tended to confine their responses to criminal prohibitions and the police rather than the entire range of legal institutions and practices that injury cases might implicate.

Finding a satisfactory way to discuss "justice" proved especially challenging. Justice has no simple or singular meaning, even in the Anglo-European tradition, and the extreme difficulty of finding a correlative term in Thai is often overlooked. Two Thai expressions—*khwam yuttitham* and *khwam pen tham*—are usually translated as "justice." Although the dictionary definition of *khwam yuttitham* is simply "justice" (Haas 1964, 434), it has formal, institutional connotations and—significantly—was never used colloquially by any of our interviewees. Thus, *yuttitham* appears in the name of the Ministry of Justice (*krasuang yuttitham*) and the courts of justice (*san yuttitham*) and is even used in the negative, though not by our interviewees, in the colloquial expression for unjust or unfair, *mai yuttitham* (literally, "not justice"). *Yuttitham* is a compound word made up of *yutti* (to conclude or finish) and *tham* or *thamma*, which in turn derives from the Pali word *dhamma* or, in Sanskrit, *dharma*. A less institutional and more commonly used term with a related derivation is *khwam pen tham*, literally "the substance of things according to dharma," an expression that the dictionary also translates as "justice" (Haas, 253). Yet the rendering in English of all of these expressions based on the concept of *tham* or *thamma* requires some qualification. The dictionary definition of *tham* is "Buddhist teaching, righteousness, dharma" (Haas, 253). *Tham*, or *dharma*, is a fundamental concept in traditional Hindu-Buddhist thought. It refers to the teachings of the Buddha and also to a cosmic law of existence governing all substances and beings in the universe according to their intrinsic nature. It is very broad, comprising the law of gravity as well as the law of torts. Dharma implies that cosmic rules will eventually produce appropriate results for virtuous acts and for acts lacking in virtue:

PLATE 6.1 *Representation of the wheel of dharma (*thammajak*), above the main entrance to the temple complex of Wat Phrathat Lampang Luang, Lampang. (David M. Engel)*

> In external terms, *dharma* is the action which, provided it is conformable to the order of things, permits man to realize his destiny to the full, sustains him in this life, and assures his well-being after death. By its own virtue that act produces a spiritual benefit for him who has performed it, which will necessarily bear fruit in the other world. Conversely, an act contrary to *dharma*, called *adharma*, necessarily involves a sanction, a "fall" for the one who does it, which will strike him in his future existence if not actually in his present life. (Lingat 1973, 3–4)

To regard *tham*, *khwam pen tham*, or *khwam yuttitham* as simple cognates for the English word *justice* is to ignore fundamental differences between Hindu-Buddhist and Anglo-European philosophical and jurisprudential traditions.

How then to explore the concept of "justice" and its relationship to "law" in contemporary Thailand without introducing distortions and non-Thai preconceptions into the very questions we ask? At the same time, one must take into account Thailand's long exposure to concepts of law and justice that did in fact originate elsewhere and were transmitted through contacts principally with Europe, Japan, and America. Over the past several decades, such contacts have accelerated, and the dissemination of liberal legal ideology and concepts of universal rights has expanded. It would be a mistake for researchers to ignore the effects of these influences on the consciousness of ordinary Thai people, yet it would be equally mistaken to assume that such concepts have become ubiquitous and have entirely displaced dharmic and other understandings of law and justice that were long familiar in Thai communities.

Recognizing the difficulty of framing an inquiry into "justice" under these complex circumstances, the approach in our study was to elicit an injury narrative that reflected the interviewees' own words and thoughts. We did not ourselves use the words for "law" or "justice" in the initial part of our interviews. Instead, we listened carefully as the injury victims responded at length to our questions about what had happened to them, why, what they did about it, and how they perceived the outcome of their experience. We wanted to observe whether and when the interviewees themselves talked about *kotmai*, *khwam pen tham*, or *khwam yuttitham*, and we found that these terms seldom surfaced. Late in the interview we deliberately introduced the first two terms ourselves, because of their more common colloquial use, by asking the following series of questions: "When people speak of *khwam mai pen tham* (literally, the substance of things *not* according to dharma), what examples do you think of? What should a person do if he or she does not receive justice? Did you ever experience injustice? Please tell us about it. Who do you think could help you to receive justice?" This last question provided an opening for the interviewees to mention lawyers and judges as agents of justice, yet none of them did so. We then asked a few questions about their experiences, if any, with specific government offices, including the court. Then we inquired, "In what matters do you think a person should seek help from the law (*kotmai*)?" We asked them to describe the experiences of anyone they knew who had used the law and finally asked them directly, "In what situations might you yourself use the law?"

Although this approach to interviewing injury victims did not completely resolve the fundamental conceptual problems involving understandings of law and justice, it did provide the interviewees a chance to address matters in their own words and with reference to their own experiences and behaviors. The results, especially when we combine findings from our interviews and from our study of court records, provide some basic insights into the concept of justice in contemporary Thai society.

Defining Justice in Contemporary Thailand

Our search for the meanings of "justice" often took us in unexpected directions. Consider, for example, our discussion with Saikham, a forty-one-year-old civil servant who had been injured in a motorcycle accident. A lifelong resident of the city of Chiangmai, Saikham feels such a deep connection to her birthplace that she becomes anxious each time she leaves, even on a short trip: "As soon as I reach Lampang [the adjoining province], I feel empty and lonely. I miss seeing Chiangmai's mountains and trees. I'd rather go home." Yet Saikham grieves that the city that she loves so much has become ugly and polluted:

> Before, in the Mae Kha River, which is near the Warorot Market, the water was so clear and plentiful. Now, and I'm not just criticizing Chiangmai, it's changed. It's really different. Maybe it's because people have become so selfish. The water is filthy. They've polluted the environment. . . . And the exhaust fumes are everywhere. It's hard to take.

In Saikham's narrative, views of the natural and social environment are closely connected to her perceptions of widespread irresponsibility and injustice broadly defined. The pollution of the air and water betoken a general social decay and a loss of the sense of mutual obligation that formerly bound the men and women of Chiangmai together. From Saikham's perspective, the central problem facing Chiangmai is a spiritual decline precipitated by the economic, technological, and demographic changes of the late twentieth century:

> "Progress" has brought a lot of changes, but I don't especially like them. The environment and the air are bad, and the minds and spirits of the people have changed. In the old days, the people were kind and generous to one another. The true natives of this area, they cared for one another like brothers and sisters. . . . If people lived in adjoining houses

and one of them went away, the residents of the other house would watch over things. But nowadays, even if the houses are connected, sometimes people don't speak and don't know one another. People's personalities have changed.

For Saikham, justice is linked not only to a proper relationship with the natural environment but to social equality. When asked to discuss examples of injustice (*khwam mai pen tham*), she observed that the contemporary era as a whole is a time of growing injustice:

> I think that poverty and wealth are a form of injustice. Yes, poverty and wealth are injustice, because sometimes the people who have money are not good people. They aren't good. Actually, people who have no money are better people. They are more honest. But if something bad happens, sometimes the poor person becomes the victim of the rich person. For example, even when they have done nothing wrong, they are accused of being the wrongdoer. It's all because of money. That's my belief.

Saikham is not alone in defining justice with reference to broad patterns of social inequality. Ming, whose injury narrative is the subject of Chapter 7, echoed her definition and cited a specific example of injustice that he regularly encounters on the highways of contemporary Chiangmai—the haughty behavior of wealthy drivers in large cars who force less wealthy motorcycle drivers off the road.

A third example of injustice, offered by Thipha, is even broader in its scope. For Thipha and others, injustice is not only a matter of the unequal distribution of wealth; it is also evident in the failure of the market to provide even a modest profit to hardworking farmers as the cost of seeds, fertilizer, and gasoline continues to rise: "Each day we work in the vegetable and rice fields. Things are expensive, and the income we get is not very much. They aren't equal. It is not justice at all."

Responses of this kind suggest that the interviewees do not conceptualize justice and injustice in legalistic terms, or at least not in terms that map readily onto concepts of civil and political rights derived from Western liberal legalism. "Injustice" implies not just a violation of legal rights but, more broadly, a sense of imbalance and inequity in the social order and in nature. For that reason, the examples of injustice that they offer go beyond situations where wrongdoers break the law; they refer to experiences of economic or social disparity and even to situations in which rich people flaunt their wealth and power by driving arrogantly and forcing poor people off the road. "Justice" does not imply narrow legal victories but, more broadly, a restoration of balance and harmony. This is not an outcome that most people in contemporary Thailand associate with litigation.

Obtaining Justice

In a society profoundly influenced by Buddhism, one would expect that concepts of justice would reflect Buddhist teachings. In the past, particularly for the large proportion of Thailand's population who live in rural settings, Buddhism was part of a syncretic mix that also included animism, Hinduism, and other "non-Buddhist" elements, all combined into "villagers' Buddhism" (see Chapter 3). Ideas about justice were filtered through this village-level belief system, and justice could be pursued through a form of customary law that drew on it. Yet, as we have seen, villagers' Buddhism has begun to lose its coherence and its hold on the thoughts and deeds of contemporary Thais, and new forms of Buddhist practice have emerged. If Buddhism is now delocalized and disconnected from customary practices, how should justice be defined, and how can it be pursued?

For Saikham, the solution to Chiangmai's problems is to be found in a "pure" form of Buddhist practice. Whenever possible, she leaves her family for ten-day retreats during which she is ordained as a Buddhist nun. When her wrist was broken in a traffic accident, she believed that her injurer could also be improved by learning a more responsible and moral way of life. Her accident was caused by the careless driving of an uneducated teenager who was fascinated by big, flashy motorcycles. Rather than trying to force his relatives to pay compensation on his behalf, Saikham abandoned her monetary claims and cooperated with a criminal prosecution resulting in a suspended sentence, court supervision, and a requirement that the boy return to school. Saikham expressed complete satisfaction with the outcome, although she received no personal benefit from it. She saw her case as an opportunity to redirect one soul away from the spiritual decay of contemporary Thailand and toward the traditional values of prior generations:

> I didn't want him to have to face anything really bad in jail and wherever. I was satisfied that he received a two-year suspended sentence. That's a pretty long time, and he will have to report in, he'll have to do well and behave in a socially useful way. So I was satisfied. And he will also have to continue his education. . . . I repaid my karma. I'm not trying to get even. Maybe this is an old-fashioned way of thinking.

Although by chance the criminal justice system proved consistent with Saikham's broader conception of "justice," she had no confidence in the court system as a general matter. Justice for her, and for others, is elusive:

> In this day and age, if you can avoid [injustice] you should. Don't go near someone you think is dangerous. Don't get involved with them. . . . Today, you can't find a way to fight back (laughs). But I think there must be a way. I just haven't found it myself. I have never seen it.

Chom, a laborer, echoed Saikham's distrust of the Thai legal system, observing bitterly that the law is not there for people like himself in the "outer circle" (*rop nok*) of society, but only for wealthy people or government officials. There is no way for people like himself to obtain justice. Both law and justice are, Chom states, strictly for others and are completely irrelevant to his life.

Thipha, who illustrated injustice in the preceding section by citing the inability of farmers to make a profit, agreed with Chom's views. For her the possibility of obtaining justice is a distant and perhaps unattainable goal:

> I don't know what else to do, just continue like this. One day, I will get justice. That's how I think about it. One day, I will get it. I just keep on. I don't know what else we can do now. Since I was born, since I was a small child, I have worked in the gardens and fields. I don't know what else I could do. I don't have much education. There is nothing else I could do.

After offering very broad and comprehensive definitions of justice and injustice, most interviewees went on to observe that the person who experiences injustice nowadays can do very little about it. In the short run, at least—or on the mundane, material plane of existence—people with greater wealth or status cannot be challenged. Formal legal institutions are almost never seen as instruments to attain justice. The courts are in the hands of government officials who have great power but cannot, according to the interviewees, be trusted to provide justice to ordinary people. Dao, for example, refers to government officials as *khon mi si*, literally "people with colors," alluding to their official uniforms. Dao was injured by an ambulance whose driver wore a uniform, and she was later interviewed by police, prosecutors, and other government officials in uniforms. She feels they were rude to her and actually threatened to make her the wrongdoer rather than the victim. Dao concludes that "people with colors" stick together, and the legal system is more likely to produce injustice than justice:

> People with colors have . . . more of an advantage than we do. They work at the same place. They know each other. We go to them, and we want them to help, but they don't help us. We don't get anything from them. Instead, they turn around and ask us angry questions.

> They should give us justice. . . . But at that time, I didn't have anyone who would help me. I was there alone. I thought, what can I do? I wanted them to give me justice, but they didn't give me any justice at all.

Many other interviewees agreed with Dao that "people with colors," including the civil servants who run the court system, are part of the problem of injustice and not part of the solution. They did not believe that the courts were a means for ordinary people to obtain justice in contemporary Thai society.

Was dissociation between justice and the legal system simply a reflection of social class and extreme disparities in wealth? Our interviews suggest that it is not only poor people in Thailand who reject the use of law in injury cases. Two of the wealthiest interviewees in our study, Prayat (discussed in the next section) and Suwit (discussed in Chapters 3 and 4), both insisted that injury victims should respond with selflessness and forgiveness. Neither Prayat nor Suwit considered himself a powerless or impoverished social outsider, yet for both of them Buddhist teachings seemed utterly incompatible with recourse to the legal system. Like Chom and Dao, they considered law to be an alien and unproductive option for those who suffer injuries. Even for these two relatively wealthy men, justice is not to be found in the law but in their religious beliefs and practices.

If injury victims are nearly unanimous in rejecting law, what would justice look like in cases of this kind? What would obtaining justice entail? Several interviewees stated that justice is achieved when both parties accept the outcome, regardless of the equities of the dispute. By contrast, injustice occurs when the resolution of a dispute leaves one party angry and dissatisfied, even though the outcome by some objective measure might be considered fair or legally correct.[1] The imbalance or perturbation that is so profoundly characteristic of injustice can be corrected only when both sides feel satisfied.

One interviewee provided a glimpse of a just outcome in an injury case. Manit, a fifty-one-year-old carpenter from a rural background, was injured in a highway accident. One evening, the injurer came to Manit's house with a group of his friends and relatives. They engaged in a long discussion with Manit's friends and relatives. Neither the village chief nor the police were involved in these group discussions. Manit's side suggested the payment of 5,000 *baht* to cover his medical costs and lost wages. The other side responded that their man was poor and couldn't afford such an amount. In the end, they settled for 3,000 *baht* (at that time, approximately $150). Manit and his supporters empathized (*hen jai*) with the other driver and felt strongly that he had behaved well in coming to Manit's house to work things out. The outcome, in Manit's view, illustrated how justice could be obtained. Both sides felt satisfied by the process, even though Manit recognized that he had not received adequate compensation for his injury.

Thipha's case led to a similar result and provides another illustration of a just outcome. Injured by a careless driver, she and her husband lost nearly 30,000 *baht* in medical expenses, travel costs, and lost income. Yet when her husband negotiated with the other driver at the police station, he saw that the injurer was poor and felt sympathy for him. The two men agreed on a settlement of 4,800 *baht*. The next day, the other driver appeared with only 3,000 *baht*, which was apparently all he could beg or borrow to pay the injury costs. Thipha's husband immediately accepted this amount, telling Thipha: "He was crying. I was soft-hearted. I got 3,000; that's enough. It's better than nothing." Thipha agreed, saying, "I felt sorry for him. He was an old man. He was over fifty, and he had nothing. He and his wife were both old. They couldn't find the money. . . . Giving that much was enough." Significantly, Thipha believed that she, like Manit, had obtained justice despite the paltry sum she and her husband received from their injurer:

> Yes, I did receive justice. Both sides were able to agree. That is justice. The police officer didn't side with one party or the other. He mediated so that it was equal. It was justice. He didn't favor either side.

The examples of obtaining justice recounted by Manit and Thipha involved settlement agreements between parties who were both poor. In those cases, justice can be obtained when both sides behave properly and commit themselves honestly to a negotiated resolution. Such cases are distinguishable from Dao's injury, in which an ordinary person on one side was opposed by "people with colors" or other wealthy and powerful individuals on the other. In cases marked by social inequality, justice is less likely to be achieved. Several interviewees, however, did cite a supposedly well-established traffic "rule" that the driver of a big car must always pay compensation to the driver of a smaller vehicle, regardless of who is in the right. One interviewee claimed to have read this rule in a police manual.[2] Even if such a redistributive custom exists, everyone nonetheless agreed that a wealthy or powerful injurer has an enormous advantage and can prevail in cases where he or she denies responsibility. Indeed, invoking the law against a more powerful adversary is very dangerous. Money and influence can make an innocent plaintiff appear to be in the wrong, and the claimant may end up being punished him- or herself. When the other side has greater wealth and power, it is prudent not to use formal legal institutions to assert a claim.

If our interviewees never cited the courts as a means to obtain justice, did they think there were other institutions to which a claimant might turn? Several interviewees expressed the opinion that justice was more likely to be obtained through the mass media than through the judicial system. Tawan, for example, described a run-in with a policeman who stopped Tawan on his motorcycle and cited him for driving without registration papers. In Tawan's view, this was clearly a technicality because few drivers carried these documents with them; and, in any case, Tawan immediately went to his house just a few blocks away, got the papers, and showed them to the officer. He then made the *wai* gesture of respect three times and asked the officer to disregard the minor infraction. Ordinarily, he believed, such a gesture should be sufficient to end the matter. The officer, however, refused and issued a ticket. Tawan was both frustrated and humiliated. He believed that the officer had expected a bribe and had shown disrespect for Tawan, who was a "mere" truck driver and day laborer and had little education.

After stewing about the incident for several days, Tawan went to a friend who worked for a national newspaper. His friend wrote up the incident as an example of police harassment, and he mentioned Tawan by name. After the article was published, the policeman called the newspaper to complain. Subsequently a national television news team came to Chiangmai and set up a concealed camera at the same intersection. Their documentary showed that police officers routinely stopped drivers and forced them to pay bribes for minor infractions. The story attracted attention throughout Thailand and led to a new policy requiring the police to make a public announcement before initiating a campaign to force drivers to show documentation.

Tawan is very negative about the legal system, the police, and the use of law to obtain justice. Nevertheless, he believes ordinary people like himself can occasionally fight back through the media and can achieve justice even in cases involving powerful adversaries. His own use of the media, in his view, proves the point.

Justice and Karma in Injury Cases

Few of the interviewees felt that their own cases had been resolved justly, and none of them mentioned courts and lawyers as a likely means to obtain justice. The best way to achieve justice is to negotiate respectfully and agree on an outcome that satisfies both parties, as Manit and Thipha had done. Yet, as we have seen, the transformation of Thai society has tended to make such negotiations more difficult than in the past and to prevent respected authority figures from serving as mediators or from invoking village customary law and the sanctioning power of the local spirits. Only one of the interviewees in our study was injured by a fellow villager, and most of them viewed their cases as falling outside the reach of any viable system of customary law.

Although village customary law has become ineffective, nearly all interviewees still cited Buddhism to explain what had happened to them and to justify their response to what they perceive as wrongdoing by the injurer. Buddhism in the abstract, separated from the efficacious local remedy systems to which it was formerly linked, appeared to them to counsel injury victims to absorb the harm without any aggressive attempt to obtain compensation. Those who attempted to follow Buddhist teachings were willing to settle for smaller payments than they thought they deserved. In many cases, they received nothing at all from their injurers. They explained such outcomes by pointing to their own karmic responsibility for the harm and by emphasizing their pursuit of a virtuous course of conduct as defined by Buddhist doctrine. In the end, they maintained, karma will ensure that justice prevails, although it may take some time. If not in this lifetime, then in a future life, the consequences of the injurer's action will be apparent. In the meantime, the injury victim must observe the Buddha's teachings, follow the eightfold path,[3] and respond to wrongdoing with forgiveness, generosity, and compassion.

Our interviews are replete with this type of reasoning as a response to wrongdoing. Karma and Buddhist belief were cited again and again as justifications for absorbing the injury while receiving little or no compensation from the injurer. For example, Prayat, the agricultural extension worker discussed in Chapter 4, refused to accept even the insurance payments available through the other driver's liability policy. He observed that the people of Lanna tend to seek justice through harmony and reconciliation. Trained in morality and ethics by renowned Buddhist teachers from childhood, they have meritorious hearts (*jai bun*) and believe that "if something is destined, then just let it go." Buddhism has molded the thinking of northern people. "It teaches people to do only good, and we carry that sort of thing in our minds at all times. That's why our society is like that." In this sense, according to Prayat, Lanna differs from other regions of Thailand where activists campaign for justice: "If they want us to march and demonstrate, we won't do it." Injured individuals like Prayat believe themselves to be the victims of injustice and think they are entitled to compensation from the other party; but if the injurer denies responsibility, they recognize that nowadays only the law can compel the payment of damages, and they are unwilling to pursue that option. Instead, they invoke Buddhist doctrine to explain why they choose to forgive the other party, accept little or no compensation, and end the karmic cycle of injury and response. In this view, Buddhism counsels against the use of law. Non-Thais might say that Buddhism in this somewhat new formulation acts as a form of "false consciousness," that it makes powerless people accept injustice in injury cases rather than resist it. Were it not for the emergence of a form of legal consciousness drawing on delocalized Buddhist beliefs, according to this view, Thais would throw off their passivity and pursue justice more aggressively. They would see more clearly that they are being deprived of their rights and that the legal system has failed them.

We think it is problematic, however, to interpret contemporary Buddhist-oriented views on the pursuit of justice and the rejection of law in northern Thailand as a mere rationalization for fear and helplessness. First, as we have suggested in Chapter 5, the emergence of this distinctive perspective on justice and law in injury cases did not occur in a time of heightened oppression, rights violations, or governmental unresponsiveness but in the relatively democratic climate of the 1990s. If contemporary views on law avoidance are merely an excuse for submission to harsh authoritarianism, why were they not more intense during the less democratic 1960s and early 1970s? Furthermore, we think it condescending to dismiss belief in karma as a form of false consciousness. Those who view karma as "false" would need to explain why rights are "real" by comparison, a culturally hegemonic task made even more difficult by European and American critical legal scholarship suggesting that rights are illusory, indeterminate, and disempowering.

Finally, it is important to emphasize that, for those who believe in the law of karma, there is nothing passive about their religious practices. Karmic responses to misfortune are *active* in the sense that they lead the individual to a deeper understanding of the reality of his or her existence and, through sometimes strenuous effort, they can transform that reality in one's current life and in future lives. According to this point of view, there are different forms of action. One is a kind of churning and ultimately destructive activity, a tit-for-tat response to wrongdoing that mistakenly views short-term, materialistic remedies or retaliatory measures as solutions to deeper problems. Such superficial responses, from this perspective, resolve nothing and merely continue the vicious cycle of injury that perpetuates suffering. A more efficacious form of action discerns the deeper causes of suffering and addresses them directly through compassionate and meritorious responses. This is not passivity. It only appears passive to those who expect or demand a very different—legalistic—kind of response.

Delocalized Buddhism in contemporary Thailand provides a powerful and comprehensive interpretive framework through which individuals can explain who they are, why they have encountered misfortune, and what they can and should do about it. Although it is a far from satisfactory solution to the problem of injustice, this form of Buddhism addresses the imperfect world in which injury victims now live. It gives them greater conrol by enabling them to confront the root cause of their suffering. It provides a discourse in which individuals can claim a measure of justice and virtue even as they abandon other kinds of claims that they could have made in times past by invoking customary remedies and, occasionally, by filing a lawsuit. Although a nonbeliever might view this as after-the-fact rationalization for those who have been deprived of rights and remedies that should be theirs, the narrators of these accounts have a different view. To them, Thai Buddhism nowadays represents a viable form of action, a prescription for positive and efficacious behavior and for spiritual fulfillment.

This is not to say, however, that our interviewees are content with the status quo. Their descriptions of justice and injustice reveal a strong undercurrent of anger and frustration. Those who suffer injuries very often believe that they are the victims of injustice, and they tend to connect their specific instances of injustice with a broader view that the economic system is out of balance, that powerful and wealthy people oppress those who lack their advantages, and that the legal system is both distant and risky for ordinary people. Buddhism, in the minds of many, offers the best way out of this intractable dilemma. It reaffirms their refusal to pursue a remedy and explains their assumption that transgressors will ultimately meet with justice, in future lives if not in this existence. But not even religion can completely reconcile injury victims to what they see as a new set of social arrangements in postglobalization Chiangmai in which they no longer have any way to obtain fair compensation when they suffer serious harm.

Conclusion

In the remembered past, when injuries tended to be localized events that could usually be mapped onto the village landscape of sacred centers, justice was both clear and attainable for injury victims. *Khwam pen tham*, meaning the substance of things according to dharma, suggested to villagers that conflicts should be resolved in accordance with local belief systems. Buddhism, in combination with non-Buddhist beliefs and practices, provided a framework for customary remediation procedures that were familiar to all villagers. Mediation of injury cases by respected authority figures provided a mechanism for implementing such practices. Typically, injury cases could be resolved through the agreement of the parties, leaving both sides satisfied. This was understood to be a tangible form of justice.

Resort to the legal system, as we have seen, was relatively rare; yet it did occur in some instances, usually as a means to impose or enforce customary arrangements. Although courts and lawyers were viewed with great apprehension and even distrust, it could not be said that such outcomes were unjust as long as they were merely extensions of local arrangements. When the courts were used as an ultimate sanction for customary law, they could be associated to that extent with justice.

In contemporary Chiangmai, however, concepts of justice have changed, and the legal system appears less likely to be associated with justice in the minds of ordinary people. Perceptions of justice are delocalized and are described in terms of general religious doctrine rather than conformity to customary laws and belief systems. Justice in the contemporary sense has to do with balance and equality in the social order and not with the narrow and legalistic resolution of particular wrongs. Courts are obviously incapable of dispensing justice in this broader and more abstract sense, and it did not even occur to our interviewees to mention the courts when asked where a person could go to get justice. Instead, they expressed doubt that ordinary people could obtain justice at all, at least in the short term, although a few did express faith in the mass media as providers of justice in some instances. On the whole, however, the interviewees responded to concerns about justice with a faith that karma would eventually distribute rewards and punishments in this lifetime or the next.

In their general observations about justice and how to achieve it, the interviewees made it clear that they now perceived law and religious belief to be fundamentally incompatible. They believed that a virtuous— and therefore *efficacious*—response to wrongdoing required them to avoid legal action and instead to adhere to the teachings of the Buddha. By doing so, they might forego their legal rights, and they might even forego the compensation to which they felt entitled, but they would resolve the root cause of their suffering and would ensure that the conflict would not continue to disrupt their lives and the lives of their children. Piety, compassion, generosity, and selflessness might lead to justice even if the law does not.

7

Ming's Injury Narrative

MING DOESN'T LOOK AT THINGS the way "old people" do. A twenty-two-year-old power line repairman, heavyset, with a dark complexion and long hair, Ming tells us that his views are those of a "new generation." He doesn't care much about the traditional northern Thai beliefs of his parents and grandparents. He is detached, even disdainful, in his comments about such beliefs. His favorite expressions, repeated throughout the narrative, are *choei choei* (makes no difference to me), *mai khoi sonjai* (I couldn't care less),[1] and *thammada* (ordinary, nothing special). Ming's comments about social practices in Chiangmai are terse and sometimes sarcastic, but when he is drawn out it becomes apparent that he knows quite a bit more than he likes to reveal. Beneath the cool and insouciant pose of this representative of a "new generation," there are lingering attachments to customary beliefs that influence Ming's attitudes and behavior in unexpected ways.

Ming lives with his wife in a new neighborhood where other industrial workers have settled on the outskirts of the city of Chiangmai. According to his description, nothing about his rented home, his lifestyle, or his everyday behavior connects him to the customary practices of northern Thailand. He wears no religious amulets on gold chains around his neck. He participates in none of Chiangmai's traditional celebrations or rituals except the Songkran Festival (traditional Thai New Year), which he views merely as an occasion to drink with his friends. He has no household shrine. There used to be a spirit house in his yard, but his uncle got drunk and kicked it down. Ming didn't care, because "The people in our house are modern Thais. We don't especially believe in this sort of thing." Ming notes that nothing bad happened as a result: "*Choei choei* (makes no difference to me)."

Ming's childhood memories, however, paint a very different picture. His parents were devout and maintained a household shrine to the Buddha as well as propitiating the household and village ancestral spirits. In fact, Ming belonged to a family in which women had long served as spirit mediums, passing the role from mother to daughter. The female spirit medium used a ceremonial bowl to receive the ancestral spirits (*phi ban* or *phi puya*) who would speak through her. When there is no female descendant to play this role in a family, then the bowl is overturned and the practice discontinued. In Ming's family, the line of female spirit mediums ran out when it came to his generation: He has no sisters. Why couldn't a male, such as Ming, serve instead? "I don't know. Because my generation couldn't care less about this (*mai khoi sonjai*)."

Ming acknowledges that spirits and spirit worship had been of paramount importance for his parents' and grandparents' generations. In the village where he grew up, there was a shrine to the village guardian spirit where all the villagers worshipped whenever there was a festival or a holy day. Ming has no interest in such practices now—"We go to the (Buddhist) temple instead." During his childhood, malicious ghosts were associated with particular trees where people had died or been murdered. Ming remembers that people sometimes saw ghosts near those trees, and individuals might become sick and die if they passed nearby without showing proper respect. To protect against such dangers, the villagers would tie a colorful cloth around the tree and perform a propitiatory ritual in which they presented an offering tray with clay figures, fruit, cigarettes, and other objects. He recalls one instance in which this ritual was insufficient to appease the ghost, and the mishaps continued until a Buddhist monk was brought to the tree to pray and make merit. The combination of animist and Buddhist protective measures proved powerful enough to remove the danger.

Later, the ghosts in Ming's home village simply disappeared as the human population expanded:

> The villagers kept bringing their relatives to occupy the land where the trees had stood. That area got filled with people, and they kept building more houses. It was always expanding. Nowadays there aren't any ghosts. They're finished.

The ghost-ridden areas have given way to development, and the new residents have no fear of retaliation by supernatural forces in any form. At times they seem to flout the old concerns about dangerous ghosts:

> People have even built houses in graveyards. Undertakers even use coffin lids to make the walls of their houses!

Ming's parents still propitiate the ancestral spirits and the ghosts, but for Ming these practices seem largely irrelevant. The trees have been cut down, the ghosts associated with them have disappeared, the spirit bowl has been overturned, and only Buddhism remains more or less a constant. In the transition from his childhood in the village to his current adult life in an urban working-class neighborhood, Ming's perspective changed considerably. His current point of view is evident in his account of injuring and then reinjuring his leg.

A Soccer Injury

> I was out playing soccer, and my ankle got twisted and began to swell up. It got so swollen that I went to see a doctor. He X-rayed the ankle and said it wasn't anything. It wasn't broken. It was just sprained. He gave me some medication to apply to my ankle for one or two weeks. After that, I went back to playing soccer.
>
> Well, about two weeks later I was back playing again. I played for three or four days. My ankle gave me pain when I played. [That day] it was even hurting at 4 P.M., when we were just getting started. We played until 6 P.M. or so. It was time to go home, and people began to leave. I was about to go myself, and I was dribbling the ball while I was running pretty fast. And my leg, it was painful at the time and didn't have much strength. Just then my friend ran into me from behind. Where he ran into me, there just happened to be a hole in the ground. I fell into the hole, and my leg twisted out to the side.
>
> I felt that my leg was broken for sure, because it was crooked. My ankle was crooked. . . . When I fell, the joint got twisted, and it

broke. My leg still hurt at that time from the first accident, and then it broke. . . .

The hole wasn't especially deep. It was just an ordinary depression. As soon as I fell, I couldn't move the leg. I had to lift it like this [lifting it with his hands]. If I just put my hand on it, the leg would shake even though I wasn't trying to move it.

It was shaking. It was hanging down all stiff and swinging back and forth. My friends were supporting me. They had a motorcycle come onto the soccer field. I was wearing a shin guard, and I used it to hold ice on the injured spot. That really made it hurt. It was excruciating. It hurt all the way home. Once I got home, the neighbors got a *tuk tuk*[2] to race me to the hospital. I had to use my hand to hold the leg up the whole way. It just hung down. And it was painful when it went down because the leg would hurt and shake.

When I got to the hospital, I waited for a doctor. There were a lot of patients then, and I was in a lot of pain. It took more than an hour before he got to me. After he examined me, I had to get some X-rays. When he examined me, the doctor grabbed me. He wasn't feeling the pain himself! He twisted my leg too much. I was already hurting, and then he twisted it some more. That was really something! (laughs).

Then they put me in a hospital room. When the X-ray was ready, the doctor looked at the film and told me they had to manipulate it again to try to get it back in place. The doctor looked at the film first, then he came and told me. So I got myself ready for it. The doctor said he would give me an injection, but I said that he didn't have to. So then the doctor twisted it again. It hurt like crazy. Each time he did something the pain was so strong! After the doctor finished, he put my leg in a splint. He put it in a splint, and then I went to lie down [in a hospital room]. I lay there, and they applied ice bags for about three nights.

At first, I asked if my wife could stay with me, but they said she couldn't. That was their rule. . . . When I first stayed there, I was afraid. I wasn't afraid of ghosts. It wasn't like that. I was afraid, I was afraid of being alone. But everyone at the hospital was good to

> me. They checked on me all the time. They really treated me well the
> whole time.
>
> I haven't seen the other guy since the injury.

Ming professes some attachment to Buddhist practices and beliefs.
He was ordained as a Buddhist monk for a short time—less than three
weeks—when he was seventeen or eighteen years old, prior to his mar-
riage. He did this because his uncle had convinced his father and mother
that it would be a good idea. But when asked why a young man should
be ordained, Ming responds, "I don't know." Does he think that by doing this he will make merit for his parents? "I kind of do and kind of
don't believe that. My father and mother never said this, but I heard old
people at home say it."

If Buddhism remains somewhat important to Ming, the traditional spirit-based practices of northern Thailand hold no interest at all. Yet
he remembers from childhood the ceremonies performed by older villagers at the shrine of the village guardian spirit. He also recalls that when
people became sick, they would consult a traditional healer (*mo mŭang*)
who would go into a trance and have a vision to reveal which ghost or
spirit caused the illness:

> If you knew that the person had encountered a spirit, you had to
> go to the woman we call a *mo mŭang*.[3] You have to ask the *mo mŭang*
> to have a vision. She will become possessed by the spirit. Once they
> know where the sick person met the spirit, they have to present an
> offering at that place. They have to offer whiskey and chicken. They
> have to make an offering. I've seen them do this.

Ming had personal experience with traditional healers when he
was ill as a child. Does he believe in their efficacy? "*Mai khoi sonjai* (I
couldn't care less). I don't think it helps. I don't believe it. . . . If I'm not
well, it's better to go and see a doctor."

Despite his skepticism, Ming tells us about a neighbor who drives
a *tuk tuk* for a living. When this man was injured in a traffic accident, a
medical doctor performed surgery and inserted a metal rod in his shoulder. The neighbor then went to see a traditional healer:

> The *mo mŭang* chanted magic words and blew on it.[4] He blew
> until the metal rod came out. There was no need for surgery to re-

move it. The metal rod actually came out by itself. I didn't see it, but they told me about it.

If the traditional healer was so helpful to the neighbor, did Ming consider similar treatment for himself when he had a metal rod implanted in his leg? "I don't believe in this. That's why I didn't go to see the *mo müang*."

Ming also expresses familiarity with traditional practices involving unnatural deaths (*tai hong*). He describes the ritual (*sut thon*) to scoop up the spirit of the person who died under unusual or violent circumstances and return it to the corpse to prevent the spirit from becoming a dangerous ghost that will cause further injury or death. "The old people say that if you don't do this, the spirit of the dead person won't have a home. It will have a bad passage. The spirit will wander around all the time. But I don't know much about this. All I know is what I've just told you." After performing the ritual, the officiant places mounds of sand at the spot of the accident and plants red flags to warn passers by that a ghost may attack them and exchange their spirit for its own. When Ming sees those flags, does he feel afraid? His answer reveals some residual respect for the power of the ghosts, accompanied by his usual ironic detachment:

> You have to be careful. You have to believe some of this nowadays. But I don't believe a lot of it because accidents can happen to us anytime. Sometimes they happen when there's no red flag. You could simply fall over and kill yourself.

Negligence as a Cause of Ming's Injury

> It was mostly negligence. It was my own negligence. Mine and my friend's. Because when I was playing I wasn't being careful. And my friend came from behind, so I couldn't really see him. And my friend was goofing around, just in a friendly way. If my friend hadn't run into me . . .
>
> At that point, we were about to stop playing because it was getting dark. We were getting ready to stop. Why did we keep playing? It was almost dark, and we kept playing.
>
> Well, I guess [my negligence and my friend's negligence] were equal. When I was injured in the first place, if I hadn't gone back and played after less than two weeks, if I'd waited for a longer time, like

one month until the pain was gone and my leg was stronger, then I could have played. I might not have been injured.

For my friend, I mean he was just goofing around more than I was. He wasn't being very careful. He overdid it.

I'm not mad at him. I just feel *choei choei*. He probably just forgot about it. He knew I had had a serious injury. When I went back to play again, he must have thought I had recovered. But actually my ankle was still swollen.

Spirits as a Cause of Ming's Injury

I couldn't care less [about spirits]. I'm not interested in this kind of thing.

My parents didn't say much. They don't believe it was caused by spirits, because it was just a soccer accident. If it had been a traffic accident, they might have believed differently. That's how old people think. . . .

A lot of these beliefs have disappeared. In the past, the old people believed in them more strongly. If there was an accident, it must be because of the spirits. The spirits did it. But nowadays, it's just the bad things people do—their own misconduct.

Karma as a Cause of Ming's Injury

I don't especially believe in karma. I'm not interested in it. It makes no difference to me. I just don't care.

Choei choei. I think accidents come mostly from ourselves.

Although Ming views his friend's negligence as a substantial cause of his injury, he never considers holding him responsible. It is apparent that Ming never considers the possibility that his friend should provide any form of traditional payment, as northern Thai customs might require. Nor does Ming consider more legalistic forms of responsibility, such as payment for medical costs or lost earnings.

Instead of looking to the other soccer player for compensation, Ming assumes that his costs should be paid through the insurance plan of his employer. He contributes about 60 to 70 *baht* per month into this plan, and he tells us that it should cover some of the costs of any injury, even if it is not work related. Here things get complicated. Ming's employer is a contractor hired to do power line repair and maintenance. Ming's understanding is that, besides having all of his medical costs covered, he is also entitled to 60 percent of his lost wages for the three months of work he missed, a total of 2,000 to 3,000 *baht* (then equivalent to approximately $50 to $75).

Yet when Ming was injured and unable to work on an earlier occasion two years previously, he filed a claim for lost wages and never received anything. The only compensation he got that time was a reimbursement for 500 *baht* of medical costs he had paid out of his own pocket. He suspects that his employer may have engaged in some form of corruption and kept the rest of the money, yet Ming was reluctant to challenge his employer for fear he might get fired. Similarly, should his employer once again fail to pay him for lost wages following his most recent injury, Ming would be inclined to forget about it rather than call attention to the impropriety and put his job at risk:

> If this turned into something where I'd have to go to the police, then I'd have to deal with that. For example, there could be a police complaint that the employer failed to act properly when I filed a claim. But if this really got my boss's attention, he might fire me!

Ming's previous injury is significant for other reasons as well. The earlier injury occurred while he was working on an electrical pole high in the air near a shrine. Knocked unconscious by an unexpected surge in the current, this member of the "new generation" experienced a vision sent by a spirit who was angry because of Ming's unwitting transgression:

A Previous Injury and a Supernatural Rebuke

> I was injured at Pa Daeng Temple, near the main hall of the temple. There was a shrine to the local guardian spirit. They told me that when I fell away from the electrical pole, I lost consciousness right away. When I came to, it was just like a dream. I thought I saw a crowd of people. [In my dream] I got up and there was a man at the shrine [i.e. a personification of the locality spirit] who came up and pointed in my face. He said, "You came here and disrespected me. You insulted me. You were above my head."[5] It turned out that when

I was working on the pole, I was higher than his head. This shrine was nearby, the shrine for the spirit.

I was working with my bare hands. I wasn't wearing my gloves, just my bare hands! I wrapped the electrical line, and when I was finished, that's when I got the shock. When I was taping it up. [The cause of the accident] was basically negligence, because at that time it was overcast, and it was raining. It's because it was too dark. The photoelectric cell, when it's dark, the current will start up by itself automatically. . . . During the day, when the sun is out and there's lots of sunshine, the electricity shuts off. But that day it was overcast and raining, so the photoelectric unit activated itself. . . .

They took me to the shrine of the locality spirit. They took me to the shrine, and I had to beg his forgiveness. The spirit spoke through the spirit medium. He said I had insulted him. I had been higher than his head. Then an old person said, "Ask his forgiveness." Because I worked for people in the village and brought them electricity, they told me what I should offer the spirit to apologize. I brought some whiskey as an offering, one bottle. The spirit medium took it and swallowed it all in one gulp! (laughs) He didn't even know enough to leave some for me.

I brought the whiskey to him as an offering, but it really didn't matter to me. My hand was red, and the skin was all wrinkled where the electricity had burned it. So he took some of the whiskey in his mouth, and he spit it on the burnt area. My hand still felt all hot. It wasn't any better. They took me to the hospital, where they did an EKG to check my heart. The doctor said I was fine. The area that was burned, that was all raw, it's still wrinkled, that's all. After two days, it swelled up with fluids.

Later on I had to go back for surgery. If the spirit medium really had some magic power, then surgery shouldn't have been necessary. My hand should have been completely healed. But instead they had to take stitches to close the wound. It had been more than a month, and the wound hadn't closed up by itself. The doctor had to stitch it up. (laughs)

[Do you think the spirit sent the dream to you?] *Choei choei* (it makes no difference to me). I think I probably just dreamed it myself.

Mai khoi sonjai (I couldn't care less). But they did say that there was a shrine for the locality spirit at that spot, and he was powerful. When I was injured, they said the spirit at that shrine was very powerful. I wasn't interested, but my mother told me to bring some whiskey and a chicken as an offering and to beg forgiveness. This was almost two years ago.

Although he is a member of the "new generation," Ming acknowledges a supernatural vision that came to him while he was suspended unconscious on the electrical pole, high above the shrine of the locality spirit. He blames his own carelessness for the accident—he wasn't wearing his gloves, and he failed to guard against the automatic activation of the photoelectric cell on an overcast day—yet he participates in a ritual of apology to the spirit medium. At the same time, he makes ironic comments about the spirit medium drinking all the whiskey and about the inefficacy of the traditional healing practice of blowing whiskey on his burnt hand.

Ming's emancipation from traditional practices is not complete. A residuum of customary beliefs also emerges in his description of the day he participated in the military draft. He was one of more than a thousand young men who were summoned to appear for the draft lottery. Those who chose red lots were drafted; those who chose black lots were exempted. Ming was told that only fifty draftees were needed, so he decided not to seek any type of deferment and instead to take the favorable odds of selecting one of the 950 black lots in the drum.

Although he analyzes the process in terms of mathematical probabilities, he also describes traditional northern Thai practices that are believed to bring good luck to potential draftees. For example, a young man is encouraged to carry a magical amulet in his mouth throughout the entire day. Ming professed to be indifferent to such practices (*choei choei*), but two years earlier his brother had kept a magic amulet in his mouth. He was so nervous that he chewed on it the whole day. By the time Ming's brother returned home, the amulet was chewed up and bitter in his mouth—and he selected a red lot anyway.

On the morning of the draft, young men in the north are also told to eat a hard-boiled egg and then walk straight out the front door without looking back. The boiled egg represents "o," meaning they will not be selected. Ming followed this practice as well. Does he believe that he chose a black lot because he ate a hard-boiled egg before leaving home?

> The guy who lives in the house next door, he ate a hard-boiled egg, too. And he drew a red lot. He got a red one (laughs). But I did it because that's what my mother wanted. She said to eat the egg, so I ate it.

Ming, a self-described "modern" young man in a society that has experienced radical change during his lifetime, has not shed all of the traditional beliefs and practices of his parents. They still affect his life at times, especially during critical moments or times of crisis. Nevertheless, his perspective is dominated by his experiences as a laborer in an increasingly industrial and technologically advanced economy. Indeed, his views of justice and injustice, as expressed in the following passage, reflect some of the tensions that have long characterized class conflict in societies around the world. It is significant that he never interprets his injuries in legal terms, nor does he consider any sort of challenge to what he suspects was corruption in handling his medical claims. For Ming, law is an ineffective and potentially dangerous option for people without money in modern Thailand.

Examples of Injustice

> I think about poor people and rich people. The rich people think that they're too big and important. Poor people aren't worth anything. When they see a poor person's face, they turn away. They just look the other way. If a poor person is riding along on his motorcycle and they are driving in a car, sometimes they just force him off the side of the road. They really do that.
>
> Poor people don't do anything [in response to injustice]. There's not much a poor person can do. They can just live their life and keep going. They just live day by day.
>
> I've run into this. I run into it every day. I'd like a rich person to be poor for a change. Let them feel what it's like. Let them feel it a little bit, those bastards who look down on poor people.

Remedy for Injustice

Most people don't care about this kind of situation. They just take life one day at a time. They don't want any big trouble. If they have a lot of problems all the time, it will get to the police and the courts. In this kind of case, a poor person doesn't have enough money. It would end up costing him his own money. That's how most people think about it.

Use of the Law

When should we use the law? I think it would be for traffic accidents, that sort of thing—if it happened when I was riding my motorcycle and a car ran into me, if the other driver insisted he was in the right and he had his insurance take care of the matter. But if it turned out that I didn't have my driver's license or something like that, then I'd be in trouble.

I don't think about this kind of thing very much. I've never used the law. I don't know how you're supposed to handle this sort of problem.

People should use the law when they have a lawsuit. That's more for the rich people, lawsuits and that sort of thing.

I don't think poor people want to bring a lawsuit. They'd rather leave things alone. They don't want to get involved with anyone else. They just try to earn a living. They don't cause any trouble.

Poor people, they don't have the money to sue. They don't have the money to hire a lawyer. [Rich people can sue] because of money, mostly. They have the money to sue.

Justice

Justice. What would be the best way to say this? I couldn't care less about this kind of thing (*mai khoi sonjai*). You could say that we don't have much justice, because, well, it's hard to say.

Justice, it should be given to both rich people and poor people. They should both get justice. Maybe there's a traffic accident, and we have to ask for justice, but the rich person pays off the police officer, and he gives a false report. That's what happens mostly.

They're not treated the same. Usually a poor person won't bring a complaint. The rich guy will just pay off the police, and the officer will take his pen and write something. The policeman's pen, it's all up to his pen. If the pen writes something else down, then all of a sudden we are in the wrong.

Rights

If you have money, if you have enough money, then you have rights.

Conclusion

WE BEGAN THIS BOOK BY ASKING what relationship globalization has to the legal consciousness of ordinary people in northern Thailand. To what extent have the dislocations and social transformations of the late twentieth century been associated with an embrace of liberal legalism in the thoughts and actions of those who suffer serious injuries? Surprisingly, we have found that ordinary people are, if anything, less likely than before to turn to the law or even to conceptualize their injuries in legal terms. For them, official law has receded. It has become more remote, inaccessible, and irrelevant and, of particular significance, it has become disconnected from custom and from the unofficial system of village-level injury remediation that was familiar to their parents and grandparents.

The previous generation lived in communities established around sacred centers, which inscribed localized identities on individuals from birth. Within those communities, respected elders and the guardian spirits themselves reminded villagers of their obligations to one another and of the norms and procedures that should be followed when injuries occurred. Consistent with their beliefs in Buddhism and the spirits, villagers had resolved injury cases by requiring payment of the cost of rituals and other forms of compensation. When injurers refused to accept their responsibility, injury victims sometimes resorted to litigation in the

Chiangmai Provincial Court to obtain the desired remedy. Litigation, although relatively rare, could potentially strengthen the community and remind its members of the norms and remedies associated with customary law.

By the end of the twentieth century, however, injury victims and injurers had begun to lose their identities as members of communities within which such customs prevailed. They lived and worked far from the sacred centers of their birth; thus, injuries tended to involve strangers and occurred in distant locations. Customary law lost its capacity to resolve injury cases under these new circumstances. Injury victims might have turned to the official legal system for a set of norms, procedures, and remedies that could replace the village-level customs of the previous generations, but they were reluctant to do so. They expressed their reluctance by citing a form of Buddhism cut off from its roots in village society. This new, delocalized religiosity seemed to our interviewees to require that injury victims recognize the karmic roots of their misfortune and respond with meritorious acts rather than an aggressive insistence on a remedy. In their minds, law was tainted not only by the sometimes suspect character of its institutions and officials but more fundamentally by its emphasis on short-term, tit-for-tat vindication rather than the Buddhist virtues of forgiveness, generosity, compassion, selflessness, and nonattachment. When injury victims asserted their interests too forcefully, they were thought to violate fundamental teachings of the Buddha rather than to enforce shared village norms and were more likely to produce further misfortune than justice.

Instead of the burgeoning spirit of liberal legalism that we expected to encounter in our interviews, we found instead a discourse of delocalized Buddhism and a renunciation of compensation in injury cases. The views expressed so consistently in the interviews found their counterparts in the litigation records of the Chiangmai Provincial Court, where there was strong evidence of a decline in injury litigation rates. Although injury victims in Chiangmai have not embraced liberal legalism, however, it would be a mistake to conclude that they have come to reject modernity itself. On the contrary, our interviewees spoke enthusiastically about some aspects of what Asad (2003, 13) calls the "project" of modernity, which "aims at institutionalizing a number of (sometimes

conflicting, often evolving) principles: constitutionalism, moral autonomy, democracy, human rights, civil equality, industry, consumerism,
freedom of the market—and secularism." Interviewees endorsed many
of these principles, especially constitutionalism, democracy, industry,
consumerism, and freedom of the market. But their approval of modernity did not include support for the law—at least not so far as injury
cases were concerned—nor did it steer them in the direction of secularism. Religion remains central to their lives, and Buddhist practices have
emerged in some sectors of Thai society with renewed vitality despite
being severed from village-level customs and beliefs.

In exploring the interconnections between globalization and legal
consciousness, it is unproductive to limit the options to a modernity
versus antimodernity binary. Instead we have examined changes in five
key elements of the legal culture: spatial and temporal frameworks; concepts of the self; community, social networks, and relationships; justice
norms and procedures; and cosmology and religious belief. We have examined each of these five elements at various points in the preceding
chapters in the course of interpreting our interview and litigation data.
By way of conclusion, we now revisit the five elements of legal culture in
a comparison of Ming's injury narrative in Chapter 7 to that of Buajan
in Chapter 1. We examine generational differences in the views of Ming
(age twenty-two) and Buajan (age thirty-nine) as they cope with similar
challenges during an era of global change. Ming, skeptical and ironic in
his conversational tone, claims to speak for the "new generation," and his
narrative may provide a glimpse of the future of law, globalization, and
legal consciousness in Thailand—and perhaps elsewhere.

Ming's life history, like Buajan's exemplifies the *spatial* dislocations
we encountered frequently in our research. He grew up in a rural community where the syncretic form of religiosity we have called "villagers'
Buddhism" (Ramitanon 2002) was supremely important—in fact his
own female forebears were well-established spirit mediums in their village. Yet Ming as a young adult has moved to a new neighborhood near
Chiangmai where other industrial workers have resettled. Like Buajan,
he lives far from the sacred center of his youth, but unlike Buajan he
never worships the guardian spirits to whom he was first presented as a
newborn. Buddhism has, for both Ming and Buajan, been delocalized;

but Ming's religiosity is more tepid. Indeed, Ming is the least devout of all our interviewees, whereas Buajan is among the most devout. *Temporal* frameworks are more obviously transformed and compressed in Ming's story than in Buajan's. Ming views his injuries in terms of the actions immediately preceding them—careless behavior on a football field or thoughtless misconduct while repairing an electrical line—and not in terms of longer karmic chains of causation stretching back to a previous existence. For Ming, these spatial and temporal transformations tend to translate injurious experiences into bounded and truncated events caused by chance or by the injury victim's own inadvertence or misjudgment. For Buajan, on the other hand, the origins and consequences of injuries extend further into the past and future and require the parties to examine more broadly the prior misdeeds of their relatives, the circumstances giving rise to malevolent ghosts, the traditions associated with ancestral spirits, and the karmic histories and trajectories of the injurer and victim.

Transformed *concepts of the self* are also evident in Ming's narrative. Tanabe (2002, 45) suggests that the "folk category of the person" in northern Thailand is "unstable," susceptible to the influence of external powers (the spirits), and not sharply individuated—hence "totally different from the modern Euroamerican folk psychology." Although this description accurately portrays Buajan's persona, Ming displays a greater degree of individuation and a diminished respect for the power of spirits. His brash expressions of disbelief contrast dramatically with Buajan's whispered and fearful references to the power of spirits. True, Ming's self-concept is far from what Tanabe would consider the Euroamerican model, and Tanabe acknowledges that the "permeable" aspects of northern Thai personhood have not disappeared completely in the era of globalization but have found other forms of expression. Beneath Ming's casual dismissal of ghosts, spirits, and even karma, we can see lingering concerns about their capacity to affect his life. Yet the still-vulnerable self that emerges from Ming's narrative is more independent and autonomous than Buajan's and is even less integrated into any network of humans and spirits.

Thus, Ming's account also illustrates more distinctly than Buajan's a profound transformation of *community, social networks, and relationships*. For Ming there is no residual sense of a group of "brothers and sisters" bound together by respect for the same village guardian spirits. His neighbors are also migrants from the countryside, and Ming knows little—and "couldn't care less"—about their customs and beliefs. Although Buajan still returns home whenever she can to observe the ceremonies and celebrations she learned in her birth village, Ming's celebrations center on drinking with his new friends in the city. Neither Buajan nor Ming describes any system of shared norms or any institutions or practices for resolving conflict in their new location. When their injuries occurred, they were not collective problems but individual misfortunes. Yet Buajan retains a sense that customary practices such as payment of *kha tham khwan* should still be observed, and she expresses frustration that her injurer cannot be held fully accountable. Ming is unfamiliar with customary village practices and regards his injuries as ad hoc problems he must analyze and resolve on his own.

Changes in *justice norms and procedures* follow from these transformations of time and space, personhood, and community. Neither Ming nor Buajan consulted a lawyer or seriously considered the use of tort or private criminal law. Ming declares that he has never used the law: "I've just relied on myself." His assertion echoes Buajan's poignant statement: "No matter how holy the law is, I have no hope of using it. I don't stand on the law, I stand on my own two legs, even though one of them is broken." Yet Buajan at least refers to the law when she observes that she could have brought a successful lawsuit against "Uncle" but chose not to. She believes that he owed her a more substantial remedy, but she cannot envision any way to enforce his obligation. By contrast, the thought of using the law never crosses Ming's mind. The law is entirely irrelevant to the injuries he has suffered. Ming believes that poor people are on their own in an increasingly atomistic society and would be foolish to get involved with the formal legal system: "I don't think poor people can get anything [from the law]. They'd rather leave it alone. They don't want to get involved with anyone else. They just try to earn a living. They don't cause any trouble." For Ming, justice is now beyond the reach of ordinary people, and rights are only for those with money: "Justice. What would be the best way to say this? I couldn't care less about this kind of thing."

As for *cosmology and religious belief,* Ming but not Buajan embodies what Nidhi Eoseewong (1998) has called the "era of disbelief not disrespect" (or, more expressively, the "era of disbelieve but don't risk sacrilege"). One of the phrases we heard most frequently during our interviews was *chửa mang mai chửa mang*—I partly believe and I partly disbelieve. Ming goes a bit further, repeatedly insisting that he "couldn't care less" about ghosts and spirits. At one point he rather daringly expresses skepticism even about the law of karma. In marked contrast to Buajan, who says that the beliefs she acquired in childhood are still "deeply planted," Ming claims indifference to the religiosity of his parents and grandparents. In his actual behavior, however, he is not exactly a prototype of the secular man in a global era. Although skeptical, he participated in a ceremony to appease the guardian spirit of a shrine whom he had unwittingly offended while working high in the air on an electrical line; and he ate a hard-boiled egg while leaving home to improve his chances of avoiding conscription. Despite his dismissive attitude, Ming still lives in a world where karma, ghosts, spirits, and other supernatural forces *might* play a role. It could do no harm to perform the appropriate rituals from time to time, and it makes his mother happy. Ming's religious beliefs and practices are a pale shadow of Buajan's piety, but something is missing from the religiosity of both Ming and Buajan. Neither can describe a set of religious practices that are not just discrete good luck charms but constitute a cosmology analogous to villagers' Buddhism. Nor can either Ming or Buajan still imagine living a religious life in relation to a sacred center that makes them part of a village-based community of believers.

We have emphasized these five key elements of legal culture throughout this book, not only in the narratives of Buajan and Ming but in the accounts of all our interviewees. They have proved useful in our exploration of the connections between social change and legal consciousness, and they have helped us to perceive a possible future of law in a transformed world. The five elements emerge somewhat differently in the injury narratives of Buajan and Ming. We should not be surprised at these differences. Despite their many common experiences during a period of intense global influences, Buajan and Ming belong to different generations with different memories of the past and expectations for the future. Yet Buajan and Ming are similar in one important respect: Their life narratives offer no indication of an intensified commitment to the ideology of liberal legalism either as a framework for interpreting experience or as a set of practices for obtaining justice. The discourse of rights and the rule of law are faintly apparent in Buajan's narrative and are entirely absent from Ming's. A strengthened association between globalization and liberal legalism is nowhere to be found in the legal consciousness of either injury victim. If Ming is, as he claims, a representative of the new generation, then liberal legalism may continue to recede in the future.

Although we have discussed our findings throughout this book in terms of the recent literature on globalization, we view our study as part of a much longer sociolegal tradition that has grappled with the problem of law and social change in many guises. Theorists from Weber and Ehrlich to the present have postulated that legal cultures and legal consciousness are shaped by the interactions of state law and nonstate law, the latter including localized, sometimes charismatic, usually unwritten, nonbureaucratic, and often explicitly religious practices for maintaining social order and resolving conflicts. In this study, our interviewees continually drew our attention to one form of nonstate law, which we have called the law of sacred centers. This set of customary norms and practices was locality based, radiating across the landscape of northern Thailand from sacred pillars, trees, and shrines. We have suggested that Thai legal culture and legal consciousness were shaped throughout much of the twentieth century by the interconnections and mutual accommodations between the law of sacred centers and the law of the state first established under King Rama V. To understand how ordinary people came to perceive and handle injuries toward the end of the twentieth century, it was necessary to consider the distinctive relationship that had evolved between state and nonstate law, each reinforcing, legitimating, and at times displacing the other.

According to our interviewees—and their views are backed by the litigation data from the Chiangmai Provincial Court—something important happened to this relationship as the twenty-first century drew near. The changes that occurred in Thai society, particularly among the two-thirds of the population who lived in rural settings, made nonstate law a thing of the past, a set of practices and beliefs distant both in time and space from the everyday lives of our interviewees. We were told again and again that this form of nonstate law had declined and now plays a far less significant role when individuals suffer injuries. Buajan, approaching middle age, still believes in the metaphysics of customary law but could no longer invoke its norms and procedures; Ming claims (almost) complete indifference and disbelief. For both of them, nonstate law exists in vestigial form at best and no longer offers a viable option for the remediation of wrongful acts resulting in injuries. With its decline, the pathway from custom to tort law has all but disappeared, and the predominant tendency is to absorb the injury rather than to seek any sort of remedy from the injurer.

It appears, then, that the expansion of liberal legalism in the thoughts and deeds of ordinary people is not necessarily a part of the globalization process, at least as far as personal injuries in northern Thailand are concerned. But would our findings have been different if we had focused on other legal fields, such as crimes, property, contracts, or even constitutional law? We chose to study personal injuries for what we considered good reasons, and our research did indeed shed useful light on legal consciousness and social change. An advantage of our focus on personal injury cases in Thailand is that they stand somewhat apart from the project of liberal legalism. The subject matter of personal injuries does not in itself require victims to frame their experiences in a discourse of rights, due process, law codes, or "rationalized" dispute resolution as might be the case for an individual who was denied a constitutional right, for example, or one who sought to enforce a commercial contract. In those instances, the very essence of the grievance is a rule-of-law violation. By contrast, it is possible to talk about A's injury of B *with or without* any reference to formal law and official legal institutions or, more broadly, to liberal legal concepts. Framing an injury narrative in terms of formal law is an option, but it is by no means unavoidable.

A focus on personal injuries offers unique advantages. It might be more difficult for researchers to disentangle the connections between globalization and liberal legalism in other areas of the law and to avoid reaching circular conclusions about the legal consciousness of those they study. Nevertheless, if researchers in the future were to find a way to conduct similar research in other fields of Thai law, we suspect that they might very well reach conclusions similar to ours. We would not be surprised to learn that the decline of official law in the consciousness of ordinary people extends beyond the realm of personal injuries. Furthermore, it is quite possible that this dissociation between globalization and liberal legalism is not confined to Thailand. We think these questions can profitably be pursued through fieldwork that explores the views, experiences, and narratives of ordinary people. The inexorable advance of liberal legalism in a globalized world should not simply be assumed. There is value, moreover, in trying to devise new sociolegal research methods capable of seeking answers without the unconscious tilt that has characterized much of the work in this field and has led to self-fulfilling predictions about the connection between globalization and liberal legalism—or the purported rejection of modernity by so-called religious fundamentalists.

Researchers who study law in the era of globalization are naturally drawn to instances in which law is active, or is actively rejected, rather than situations in which it lies dormant or is simply ignored. Unfortunately, legal scholars do not share Sherlock Holmes's fascination with the dog that does not bark. Yet the inactivity of law in the lives and consciousness of ordinary people may be its most important feature in the current era. The dog that does not bark is precisely the phenomenon we need to study and explain. The residents of northern Thailand may speak for others around the world when they characterize the law as increasingly remote and justice in this lifetime as more unattainable than ever before. If so, it is the decline of law that demands our attention, and its absence from everyday life may be the hallmark of our age.

Reference Matter

Notes

Introduction

1. Pseudonyms are used for all interviewees cited in this book.

2. McCann (1994, 7) defines legal consciousness as "the ongoing, dynamic process of constructing one's understanding of, and relationship to, the social world through use of legal conventions and discourses." Legal consciousness, as we use the term, has important implications for the role and legitimacy of formal legal institutions and actors, even when they are not explicitly invoked. It refers not only to situations in which individuals perceive the relevance of law to their experiences but also to situations in which other interpretive frameworks predominate. Legal frameworks are related to alternative interpretive frameworks differently in different kinds of social and cultural environments. Elsewhere, we have observed that "Law is one of the elements that constitute the categories and routines of everyday life; and, in turn, these very categories and routines—and the individuals who participate in them—give form and meaning to the law. . . . The term 'legal consciousness' is now widely used to characterize this two-way process and the behavior and cognition of the social actors who participate in it" (Engel and Munger 2003, 11).

3. We use the term *injury* to refer to tangible bodily harm. This definition corresponds to the meaning of the Thai term, *bat jep* (injury or wound, according to Haas 1964, 288), which was most frequently used by the interviewees in this study to describe the harm they had suffered that required medical treatment. We recognize, however, that the concept of injury in Thai culture is complex and might reward further study. It will be apparent in some of the quotes we present that "injury" is closely connected to "illness" in the minds of the interviewees. When a malevolent ghost takes action against a human, injury *or* illness *or both* may result. Furthermore, as we hope to make clear, the distinction between bodily injury and spiritual or psychological harm is tenuous at best in some of these injury accounts because most bodily injuries also affect the individual spirit essence (*khwan*) and other intangible aspects of the person. Nevertheless, while we acknowledge that the concept of bodily harm may lack clear boundaries, it did provide us with a useful starting point for our fieldwork. For one thing, it corresponded to an

important colloquial term that was immediately understood by all who participated in the research. In addition, it defined a type of harm that is explicitly recognized in Thai tort law and criminal law. Furthermore, our focus on bodily injury provided us with a means to identify a group of accident victims who could participate in the interviews on which this study is based, as we will describe in the next few pages.

4. There have been a few important exceptions. See, for example, discussions of tort law issues stemming from the Bhopal disaster in Galanter 1985 and 1986 and Cassells 1996. Transnational tort litigation has captured a good deal of scholarly attention (e.g., Bloom 2001, Stephens 2002, and Shamir 2004), but the purpose of our study is to focus solely on the relationship between globalization and the use of local and national remedy systems in Thailand, not the transnational litigation of tort claims.

5. Examples of such research include Coutin 2000 and Munger 2002.

6. Whether and to what extent an injury "involves the conduct of another party" is, of course, a matter of interpretation. As we shall attempt to make clear, the role of other human and supernatural actors depends on the interpretative framework of the observer. For example, Inta undoubtedly thought his injury involved the conduct of the ghost he passed along the highway, but he might have differed from a legal observer in his assumption about the involvement of his employer (who knowingly exposed Inta to the risks associated with a defective stamping machine) or the manufacturer of the machine with a defective braking mechanisms that crushed Inta's hand. Whereas we view his accident as involving, at least to some extent, both the employer and the manufacturer, Inta himself might see things differently. In this study, we selected only those cases in which we thought it at least possible for the injury victim to view others as involved in his or her misfortune, but one goal of our interviews was to determine whether the interviewee actually held such a view. In many instances, he or she did not.

7. We conducted each interview with one or both of our two Chiangmai-based fieldwork assistants—Ms. Sutthira Foocom and Ms. Rotjarek Intachote (who are also nurses and are familiar with northern Thai language and culture). Interviews explored the personal background, life history, and belief systems of the interviewee, as well as the sequence of events connected to his or her injury and general experiences with and impressions of governmental agencies, officials, lawyers, and courts. Interviews concluded with a general discussion of "justice" in contemporary Thai society. All interviews were taped and transcribed in Thai. The translations into English are our own.

8. To explore the effects of globalization on the legal consciousness of individuals who lived in rural versus urban settings, we divided the original pool of ninety-three injured persons into two groups based on their current place of residence. The pool consisted of thirty-seven people who resided in urban locations and fifty-six who resided in rural locations. Of these, we selected for our extended interviews nineteen persons in urban locations and sixteen in rural locations. Our slightly disproportionate emphasis on urban residents reflected our discovery that this group in fact consisted of

two subcategories, lifelong city dwellers and those who had moved to urban areas from the countryside, often as a result of factors associated with globalization. We wished to understand the experiences of both of these "urban" groups as well as those who chose to remain in rural settings, and we therefore selected a greater number of urban dwellers for interviews than their proportionate representation in the original pool of ninety-three injured persons might have suggested. In addition to the urban–rural breakdown, we considered several other factors in selecting interviewees. The gender distributions of the thirty-five interviewees (twelve women and twenty-three men) reflected that of the original pool (twenty-nine women and sixty-four men). We attempted to include a range of ages because we suspected that the narratives offered by persons at different life stages might be affected by globalization in different ways (nine interviewees ranged from twenty to thirty years of age, sixteen interviewees ranged from thirty-one to forty years of age, six interviewees ranged from forty-one to fifty years of age, and four interviewees were over fifty years old). Our selection of interviewees also took into account the circumstances of their injuries. In the original pool of ninety-three injured persons, seventy were injured in traffic accidents and twenty-three in nontraffic accidents. Because the nontraffic accidents were more varied in their circumstances—and in the interpretations offered by the injured persons—we oversampled them, selecting sixteen nontraffic accident victims as compared to nineteen traffic-related accident victims. We also attempted to include individuals from different economic strata. Most were low income or unemployed. Thus, twenty-three had monthly incomes of 6,500 *baht* or less (approximately $212). Five interviewees, however, had monthly incomes of 10,000 *baht* or more (approximately $255), ranging as high as 18,600 *baht* (approximately $465). In applying all of these selection criteria, the choice of individual interviewees from the original pool of ninety-three injury victims was otherwise random, based on anonymous summaries obtained during their hospital treatment.

9. We discuss civil and private criminal injury litigation in Chapters 3 and 5.

10. We are fluent in central Thai, a dialect understood by all our interviewees. Some interviewees responded to our questions in a combination of central and northern dialects. We were able to understand most of these responses without difficulty, but occasionally we depended on our research assistants to translate particular expressions from northern to central dialect.

Chapter 1

Portions of Chapters 1 and 2 were previously published in David M. Engel, "Globalization and the Decline of Legal Consciousness: Torts, Ghosts, and Karma in Thailand," *Law & Social Inquiry* 30 (2005): 469–514.

1. Note that Buajan appears to merge the concepts of fate and karma, although their characteristics are arguably quite different (see Keyes 1977:117). At times Buajan uses the two terms interchangeably.

2. This is significant because Buajan's own leg was broken in the accident.

3. It is unclear whether this encounter with the duty officer occurred prior to her negotiations with "Uncle" or after she had signed the release at the lawyer's office.

Chapter 2

1. The name *Chiangmai* literally translates as "new city."

2. *Tai* refers to the ethnolinguistic group currently scattered throughout southern China and northern Southeast Asia. *Thai* refers to citizens of the modern state of Thailand, who are predominantly but not exclusively Tai. See, generally, Keyes (1977, 74–79) and Wyatt (1984, 1–2).

3. As Ongsakul explains, Lanna rulers were regarded locally as "king" (*jao luang* or *phraya luang*), although the Siamese considered them rulers of a tributary state, *jao prathetsarat* (129). The term *prince* might have been considered more appropriate from the perspective of the Bangkok monarchy.

4. "The resettled people often named their new villages after the places they had been forced to leave. . . . The resettlements involved all social levels, from nobles to commoners. Resettled nobles were allowed to continue to govern their own people, under the supervision of Lan Na leaders. There is clear evidence that entire resettled *mueang* kept their old cultural systems" (Ongsakul, 136).

5. Treaty between Great Britain and Siam (1874); Treaty between Great Britain and Siam (1883).

6. The figure reported by Phongpaichit and Baker is 62 billion *baht*. The conversion rate for 1990 varied monthly from a low of 25.1 *baht* per U.S. dollar to a high of 26.0. We have used the figure for December, which was 25.2 *baht* per U.S. dollar.

7. The six provinces are Bangkok, Nakhon Pathom, Nonthaburi, Pathum Thani, Samut Prakan, and Samut Sakon.

Chapter 3

Portions of Chapters 3 and 4 were previously published in David M. Engel, "Landscapes of the Law: Injury, Remedy, and Social Change in Thailand," *Law & Society Review* 43: 1–34 (2009).

1. This incident is recounted in Winichakul (1994, 34–35), who draws on and quotes the contemporary account of an English participant, Frederick A. Neale (1852).

2. We have discussed the transformation of law and political space elsewhere (Engel 1990; 1994; 2009). The construction of space within the new nation-state has been discussed most extensively by Winichakul (1994).

3. Compare Delaney, Ford, and Blomley (2001, xviii): "Boundaries *mean*. They signify, they differentiate, they unify the insides of the spaces that they mark. . . . How they mean is through the authoritative inscription of legal categories, or the projection of legal images and stories on to the material world of things" (emphasis in original).

4. Santos (1995, 468), citing and summarizing Weber's *Economy and Society: An Outline of Interpretive Sociology* (1978, 698 and 724).

5. Other specialized courts of first instance have also been established in Chiangmai, such as the Juvenile and Family Court and the Administrative Court.

6. An example is the recently enacted Products Liability Law of 2008, which appeared after this study was completed.

7. Section 59, Subsection 4.

8. A classic description of birth practices in central Thailand is provided in Hanks (1963).

9. Ramitanon (2002, 33–34) emphasizes the distinction between this integrated and socially embedded type of Buddhism, which he calls "Villagers' Buddhism," and the more abstract and doctrinal strain that he terms "Orthodox Theravada Buddhism."

10. Each human possesses thirty-two *khwan* located in various parts of the body (Phaya Anuman Rajadhon 1963; Nimmanhaemin 1978, 106; Chetphatanawanit 2003, 63). Because the Thai language does not require a distinction between singular and plural nouns, in common speech *khwan* could refer to one or all of the thirty-two spiritual essences in the human body. Because English requires us to avoid this ambiguity, however, we discuss *khwan* as if it were a singular noun.

11. Such rituals were called *thon winyan* or *sut thon*. They provide another illustration of the seamless merger of Buddhism and spirit-based practices.

12. "*Sati* denotes self-watchfulness, which is to distance or detach oneself from one's thoughts and actions and so attain mental and moral equilibrium. *Sati* or mindfulness is the basic Theravada meditative practice, usually developed by the practice of observing the inward and outward breath" (Jackson 2003, 135).

13. Compare French (1995, 75): "In Tibetan Buddhism the mind, like a wild elephant racing through the jungle, must be tamed through ethical actions, meditation, understanding, and habitual calm, clear thought. The liberated mind achieves enlightenment; the afflicted mind creates conflict."

Chapter 4

1. A detailed examination of injury litigation, documenting an apparent decline in the injury litigation rate over the past four decades, appears in Chapter 5.

2. Yü (2001) traces the historical origins of the "Goddess of Mercy" in India and China and its evolution and transmission throughout Asia.

3. Highland peoples, or "hill tribes," are predominantly non-Buddhist. According to the 2000 census, which counted mostly lowland peoples, 92.2 percent of Chiangmai's population was Buddhist, and 6.0 percent was Christian (National Statistical Office of Thailand 2000; retrieved on August 3, 2009, from: http://web.nso.go.th/pop2000/finalrep/cheingmaifn.pdf).

Chapter 5

Portions of this chapter were previously published in David M. Engel, "Globalization and the Decline of Legal Consciousness: Torts, Ghosts, and Karma in Thailand," 30 *Law & Social Inquiry* 30: 469–514 (2005).

1. For example, Hurst (1956, 11) asserted that the law's "procedures and compulsions were inextricably involved in the growth of our market economy." Addressing the increased flow of litigation in the Wisconsin Supreme Court during a time of dramatic economic expansion, Hurst (1964, 154) wrote that it was "in well-defined relation to the growth of the economy."

2. The filing of a lawsuit should be distinguished from a trial. In Thailand, as in other countries, most personal injury lawsuits are settled and withdrawn after they are filed but before they can be tried and adjudicated.

3. The following discussion draws heavily on Saks (1992), which is still the most cogent and comprehensive analysis of litigation rates in general and personal injury cases in particular.

4. In 2000, New York's population was 18,976,457 (U.S. Census Bureau 2009) and 78,323 tort cases were filed (Court Statistics Project 2006, Table 4).

5. Michigan's population in 2000 was 9,938,444 (U.S. Census Bureau 2009) and the number of tort cases filed in Michigan that year was 22,243 (Court Statistics Project 2006, Table 4). Ohio's population in 2000 was 11,353,140 (U.S. Census Bureau 2009) and the number of tort cases filed was 30,197 (Court Statistics Project 2006, Table 4).

6. Maine's population in 2000 was 1,274,923 (U.S. Census Bureau 2009) and court administrators reported the filing of 1,253 tort cases in that year (Court Statistics Project 2006, Table 4). Maine is ranked as the second most rural state in the United States with 59.8 percent of its population living in rural areas. Vermont is the most rural state but does not report its tort litigation figures (U.S. Census Bureau 2009).

7. Arkansas is the sixth most rural state in the United States, with a rural population of 47.5 percent (U.S. Census Bureau 2009). Its total population in 2000 was 2,673,400 (Id.), and its reported tort case filings totaled 4,401 (Court Statistics Project 2006, Table 4).

8. Although the Ministry of Public Health makes available certain annual statistics about accidental injuries, such figures fluctuate wildly from year to year and are far from reliable tallies of all such injuries that occurred in the province during a given year.

9. The vagaries of official statistics in Thailand are apparent even in this relatively reliable source of data. As the chart suggests, figures are unavailable for two years, 1986 and 1987. Government archivists explained to us that the absence of statistics for these two years probably resulted from budget shortfalls in the province that disrupted the usual reporting process.

10. Numerous other private criminal actions were litigated for offenses that did not involve personal injuries.

11. Private health insurance played little role throughout this period. According to Supakankunti (2000, 85), only 1.6 percent of the total Thai population in 1992 had private health insurance, a figure that increased very slightly to 2.0 percent by 1995. It is safe to assume that such insurance was purchased by a very small number of affluent urban residents and not by the ordinary people of Chiangmai.

12. A major development in social health insurance, the so-called Thirty Baht Plan offering nearly universal coverage, was not enacted until 2002 and therefore came after the period of time we need to examine (see, e.g., Towse, Mills, and Tangcharoensathien 2008).

13. Of the one-third (thirty-one persons) in our sample who were likely to have some form of work-related health benefits, nearly half (fourteen persons) were civil servants and were presumably covered by the Civil Servant Medical Benefit Scheme discussed below.

14. A list of names of all attorneys registered in the province of Chiangmai in 2001–2002 was provided to the authors by the Lawyers Association of Chiangmai Province.

15. According to our informants, no changes had occurred in the fee structures or billing practices of personal injury attorneys over this time span that might have contributed to a decline in tort litigation.

Chapter 6

1. Compare the Tibetan emphasis on complete agreement and acceptance of an outcome by both parties in a dispute (French 1995).

2. We are skeptical and could not verify this claim.

3. The Eightfold Path is the fourth of the Four Noble Truths enumerated by the Buddha in his sermon at Benares (summarized in Sivaraksa 1992, 63): "Suffering; the Cause of Suffering, namely desire or craving; the Cessation of Suffering; and the Way to the Cessation of Suffering, namely the Eightfold Path—Right Understanding, Right Mindfulness, Right Speech, Right Action, Right Livelihood, Right Effort, Right Attention, and Right Concentration."

Chapter 7

1. *Mai khoi sonjai* literally means, "I'm not especially interested."

2. A *tuk tuk*, which is a common and inexpensive taxi found throughout Thailand, is a covered three-wheeled motorcycle with a small passenger bench seat behind the driver. "*Tuk tuk*" is the sound the vehicle makes, roughly equivalent to "putt-putt."

3. As noted above, *mo müang* refers to a traditional healer. Because Thai pronouns—as well as the word *khon*, meaning "person"—are gender neutral, Ming could refer to either a woman or a man in this passage. For convenience, our translation assumes the healer was a woman.

4. Treatment by blowing is a common customary practice. The practitioner fills his or her mouth with holy water or other magical potion and blows a spray of it on the afflicted area.

5. When the spirit spoke to Ming, it used the archaic pronouns *ku* (I) and *mŭng* (you), which are ordinarily considered rude and insulting in contemporary speech. Use of these pronouns through a spirit medium makes the spirit sound both ancient and powerful.

Glossary of Thai Words and Phrases

Ayutthaya Capital of Siamese kingdom in central Thailand from 1351 C.E. until its destruction by the Burmese in 1767 C.E.

bat jep Bodily injury or wound.

baht Thai currency worth approximately $0.025 in the 1990s prior to the financial crisis of 1997.

choei choei An expression of indifference or emotional neutrality.

chŭa mang mai chŭa mang "I partly believe and partly disbelieve" (can also be expressed as *chŭa bang mai chŭa bang*).

dika court (san dika) Thailand's highest (supreme) court.

jao mae kuan im Thai version of the Chinese "goddess of mercy," increasingly popular throughout the country and associated with morality, piety, and kindness.

kamnan Elected leader of an administrative subdistrict (*tambon*) representing a group of villages.

kha tham khwan Payment for the ceremony to recall the *khwan*-soul; general term referring to payment by the injurer to the injury victim.

khon mi si Literally, "people who have colors"; refers to people who are set apart from the general population because they wear uniforms, such as the police, military, or other government officials.

khro Fate. *Sado khro* is a ceremony to "unlock" one's fate and enhance future prospects.

kotmai Law or regulation.

khwam pen tham An expression usually translated as "justice"; literally, the substance of things according to dharma. *Khwam mai pen tham* is injustice; literally, the substance of things *not* according to dharma.

khwan Flighty spiritual essence contained in every human and in some natural objects, such as mountains and rice fields. Trauma, such as injury, fright, or illness, causes the *khwan* to escape from the body.

lang sanghon Premonition or forewarning.

lanna or **lan na** Historic northern Thai region, literally "million rice fields."

mai khoi sonjai "I am not particularly interested; I couldn't care less."

monthon Historically, administrative regions (or circles) established by King Rama V, containing groups of provinces.

mo mŭang Traditional healer.

Phayap An administrative region containing the provinces of northern Thailand.

phi Ghost (referring to a specific deceased person) or spirit (referring to a supernatural being not necessarily associated with a specific deceased person). *Phi tai hong* is the ghost of an individual who died an abnormal or violent death (*tai hong*), usually malevolent and dangerous unless properly propitiated.

pho luang Northern Thai term for village chief (literally "big father").

pramat Negligence, imprudence.

pu dam ya dam Literally "black grandfather and black grandmother"; refers to the ancestral spirits associated with the household's charred clay rice pot.

ro ha Abbreviation (R 5) for King Rama V.

sati Mindfulness in Buddhist practice.

songkran Traditional Thai New Year celebration.

sŭa Guardian spirits in northern Thailand. *Sŭa ban,* for example, refers to village guardian spirits; *sŭa wat* refers to guardian spirits of a temple.

sŭp chata "Life extension" ceremony to make merit for individual or group and strengthen prospects for the future.

sut thon Northern Thai ceremony to propitiate ghost of individual who dies an untimely or violent death (*tai hong*), combining Buddhist and non-Buddhist elements.

thesaphiban The administrative system established by King Rama V to unify the Siamese polity under central control.

tham or **thamma** Thai version of dhamma (Pali) or dharma (Sanskrit), cosmic law of righteousness and justice.

tuk tuk Inexpensive and colorful three-wheel taxis made from motorcycles with narrow bench seat behind the driver.

wai Gesture of greeting, parting, and respect made by placing palms of hands together.

winyan Human soul essential to life, which departs from the body on death and continues to existence in other forms or incarnations. Sometimes used simply to refer to the ghost of a dead person.

yuttitham Justice, as in Ministry of Justice (*krasuang yuttitham*) or courts of justice (*san yuttitham*). *Mai yuttitham* is a colloquial expression meaning "unjust" or "unfair."

Names of Injury Victims Referenced in Text

Aran: Age thirty, male. Restaurant worker injured in motorcycle accident involving a young woman driving a motorcycle.

Bancha: Age twenty-nine, male. University maintenance worker who injured his back in a fall while pruning a tree.

Buajan: Age thirty-nine, female. Hotel kitchen worker struck by "old man" driving car.

Chom: Age thirty-seven, male. Worked in a restaurant owned by girlfriend, injured when his apartment was destroyed by fire caused by faulty wiring or by neighbor's incense (girlfriend was killed).

Dao: Age twenty-one, female. Noodle shop employee struck by ambulance while riding motorcycle.

Inta: Age twenty-six, male. Factory worker whose hand was crushed by stamping machine.

Jampa: Age forty, female. Seamstress whose motorcycle collided with a car driven carelessly by teenager.

Kham: Age fifty-one, male. Cleaning company employee struck by hit-and-run truck driver while he was riding his motorcycle.

Manit: Age fifty-one, male. Craftsman whose finger was partially amputated by power saw while making furniture.

Ming: Age twenty-two, male. Power company employee injured playing soccer. Previously injured while repairing power line.

Müang: Age thirty-six, male. School watchman injured by starter pedal on motorcycle.

Prayat: Age forty-seven, male. Government-employed agriculture advisor, injured while riding his motorcycle when a car passed him and then cut him off.

Saikham: Age forty-four, female. Clerk in government office injured when teenage motorcyclist disobeyed a traffic sign and struck her motorcycle.

Suwit: Age forty-five, male. University professor injured in fall from ladder.

Tawan: Age forty-two, male. Grows lychee and longan, injured when another motorcyclist ran into his motorcycle and broke his finger.

Thipha: Age thirty-eight, female. Farmer injured in motorcycle collision.

Bibliography

Amsterdam, Anthony G., and Jerome Bruner. 2000. *Minding the Law: How Courts Rely on Storytelling, and How Their Stories Change the Ways We Understand the Law—and Ourselves*. Cambridge, MA: Harvard University Press.

Anderson, Benedict. 1991. *Imagined Communities: Reflections on the Origins and Spread of Nationalism*. Rev. ed. New York: Verson.

Appadurai, Arjun. 1996. *Modernity at Large: Cultural Dimensions of Globalization*. Minneapolis: University of Minnesota Press.

Asad, Talal. 2003. *Formations of the Secular: Christianity, Islam, Modernity*. Stanford, CA: Stanford University Press.

Baker, Chris, and Pasuk Phongpaichit. 2005. *A History of Thailand*. Cambridge, U.K.: Cambridge University Press.

Baker, Tom. 2001. Blood Money, New Money, and the Moral Economy of Tort Law in Action. *Law & Society Review* 35: 275–319.

Bloom, Anne. 2001. Taking on Goliath: Why Personal Injury Litigation May Represent the Future of Transnational Cause Lawyering. In Austin Sarat and Stuart Scheingold, eds., *Cause Lawyering and the State in a Global Era*, 96–116. New York: Oxford University Press.

Bruner, Jerome. 1990. *Acts of Meaning*. Cambridge, MA: Harvard University Press.

Bunnag, Tej. 1977. *Provincial Administration of Siam 1892–1915*. Kuala Lumpur: Oxford University Press.

Cassells, Jamie. 1996. *The Uncertain Promise of Law: Lessons from Bhopal*. Toronto: University of Toronto Press.

Charoenloet, Voravidh. 1997. *Labour Standards in Thailand: The Impact of Trade Liberalisation*. Geneva: Program for the Study of International Organisation(s).

Chetphatanawanit, Khomnet. 2003. *Khwam chúa phǔnban lanna thaithot jak prasopkan khong than phuru nai thongthin [Lanna village beliefs transmitted from the experiences of local knowledgeable persons]*. Chiangmai: Social Research Institute, Chiang Mai University.

Chua, Amy. 2002. *World on Fire: How Exporting Free Market Democracy Breeds Ethnic Hatred and Global Instability*. New York: Doubleday.

Court Statistics Project. 2006. *State Court Caseload Statistics.* Williamsburg, VA: National Center for State Courts.

Coutin, Susan Bibler. 2000. *Legalizing Moves: Salvadoran Immigrants' Struggle for U.S. Residency.* Ann Arbor: University of Michigan Press.

Damrikun, Suraphon. 1999. *Lanna: singwaetlom, sangkhom, lae watthanatham [Lanna: environment, society, and culture].* Bangkok: Compact Print.

Davis, Richard. 1984. *Muang Metaphysics: A Study of Northern Thai Myth and Ritual.* Bangkok: Pandora.

de Certeau, Michel. 1984. *The Practice of Everyday Life.* Trans. Steven Rendall. Berkeley and Los Angeles: University of California Press.

Delaney, David, Richard T. Ford, and Nicholas Blomley. 2001. Preface: Where Is Law? In Nicholas Blomley, David Delaney, and Richard T. Ford, eds., *The Legal Geographies Reader,* xiii–xxii. Oxford, U.K.: Blackwell.

Dixon, Chris. 1999. *The Thai Economy: Uneven Development and Internationalisation.* London: Routledge.

Engel, David M. 1975. *Law and Kingship in Thailand during the Reign of King Chulalongkorn.* Ann Arbor: University of Michigan Center for South and Southeast Asian Studies.

Engel, David M. 1978. *Code and Custom in a Thai Provincial Court: The Interaction of Formal and Informal Systems of Justice.* Tucson: University of Arizona Press, for the Association for Asian Studies.

Engel, David M. 1990. Litigation across Space and Time: Courts, Conflict, and Social Change. *Law & Society Review* 24: 333–344.

Engel, David M. 1994. Dynastic Realms and Secular States: Introduction. *Law & Society Review.* 28: 429–431.

Engel, David M. 2005. Globalization and the Decline of Legal Consciousness: Torts, Ghosts, and Karma in Thailand. *Law & Social Inquiry* 30: 469–514.

Engel, David M. 2009. Landscapes of the Law: Injury, Remedy, and Social Change in Thailand. *Law & Society Review* 43: 61–94.

Engel, David M., and Frank W. Munger. 1996. Rights, Remembrance, and the Reconciliation of Difference. *Law & Society Review* 30: 7–53.

Engel, David M., and Frank W. Munger. 2003. *Rights of Inclusion: Law and Identity in the Life Stories of Americans with Disabilities.* Chicago: University of Chicago Press.

Engel, David M., and Eric H. Steele. 1979. Civil Cases and Society: Process and Order in the Civil Justice System. *Law & Social Inquiry (American Bar Foundation Research Journal)* 1979: 295–346.

Eoseewong, Nidhi. 1998. *Yuk samai mai chůa ya loplu [An era of disbelief not disrespect].* Bangkok: Amarin.

Ewick, Patricia, and Susan S. Silbey. 1998. *The Common Place of Law: Stories from Everyday Life.* Chicago: University of Chicago Press.

Felstiner, William L. F., Richard Abel, and Austin Sarat. 1980–81. The Emergence and Transformation of Disputes: Naming, Blaming, Claiming . . . *Law & Society Review* 15: 631–654.

Fitzpatrick, Peter. 2005. "The damned word": Culture and Its (In)compatability with Law. *Law, Culture and the Humanities* 1: 2–13.

Fitzpatrick, Peter. 2007. The Triumph of a Departed World: Law, Modernity, and the Sacred. In Austin Sarat, Lawrence Douglas, and Martha Merrill Umphrey, eds., *Law and the Sacred*, 155–183. Stanford, CA: Stanford University Press.

Foucault, Michel. 1980. *Power/Knowledge: Selected Interviews and Other Writings, 1972–1977*. Ed. Colin Gordon; Trans. Colin Gordon, Leo Marshall, John Mepham, and Kate Soper. New York: Pantheon Books.

French, Rebecca Redwood. 1995. *The Golden Yoke: The Legal Cosmology of Buddhist Tibet*. Ithaca, NY: Cornell University Press.

Friedman, Lawrence M., and Robert Percival. 1976. A Tale of Two Courts: Litigation in Alameda and San Benito Counties. *Law & Society Review* 10: 267–301.

Galanter, Marc. 1974. Why the "Haves" Come Out Ahead: Speculations on the Limits of Legal Change. *Law & Society Review* 9: 95–160.

Galanter, Marc. 1985. Legal Torpor: Why So Little Has Happened in India after the Bhopal Tragedy. *Texas International Law Journal* 20: 273–94.

Galanter, Marc. 1986. When Legal Worlds Collide: Reflections on Bhopal, the Good Lawyer, and the American Law School. *Journal of Legal Education* 36: 292–310.

Ganjanapan, Anan. 2002. Globalization and the Dynamics of Culture in Thailand. In Shinji Yamashita and J. S. Eades, eds., *Globalization in Southeast Asia: Local, National and Transnational Perspectives*, 126–141. New York: Berghahn Books.

Giddens, Anthony. 2003. *Runaway World: How Globalization Is Reshaping Our Lives*. New York: Routledge.

Haas, Mary R. 1964. *Thai–English Student's Dictionary*. Stanford, CA: Stanford University Press.

Hanks, Jane Richardson. 1963. *Maternity and Its Rituals in Bang Chan*. Data Paper No. 51, Southeast Asia Program. Ithaca, NY: Department of Asian Studies, Cornell University.

Harding, Andrew. 2008. The Eclipse of the Astrologers: King Mongkut, His Successors, and the Reformation of Law in Thailand. In Penelope (Pip) Nicholson and Sarah Biddulph, eds., *Examining Practice, Interrogating Theory: Comparative Legal Studies in Asia*, 305–339. Leiden, The Netherlands: Martinus Nijhoff.

Harvey, David. 1990. *The Condition of Modernity: An Enquiry into the Origins of Cultural Change*. Cambridge, MA: Blackwell.

Hirschkind, Charles. 2006. *The Ethical Soundscape: Cassette Sermons and Islamic Counterpublics*. New York: Columbia University Press.

Hurst, James Willard. 1956. *Law and the Conditions of Freedom in the Nineteenth Century United States*. Madison: University of Wisconsin Press.

Hurst, James Willard. 1964. *Law and Economic Growth: The Legal History of the Lumber Industry in Wisconsin, 1836–1915*. Cambridge, MA: Harvard University Press.

Hussey, Antonia. 1993. Rapid Industrialization in Thailand, 1986–1991. *Geographical Review* 83: 14–28.

Ietswaart, Heleen F. P. 1990. The International Comparison of Court Caseloads: The Experience of the European Working Group. *Law & Society Review* 24: 571–593.

Inda, Jonathan Xavier, and Renato Rosaldo. 2002. Introduction: A World in Motion. In Jonathan Xavier Inda and Renato Rosaldo, eds., *The Anthropology of Globalization: A Reader*, 1–34. Malden, MA: Blackwell Publishers.

Jackson, Peter A. 2003. *Buddhadāsa: Theravada Buddhism and Modernist Reform in Thailand.* Seattle: University of Washington Press.

Keyes, Charles F. 1977. *The Golden Peninsula: Culture and Adaptation in Mainland Southeast Asia.* New York: Macmillan.

Khamchan, Mala. 2001. *Lao rŭang phi lanna [Stories of the Lanna spirits].* Bangkok: Matichon Press.

Lingat, Robert. 1973. *The Classical Law of India.* Trans. and additions, J. Duncan M. Derrett. Berkeley: University of California Press.

Loos, Tamara. 2006. *Subject Siam: Family, Law, and Colonial Modernity in Thailand.* Ithaca, NY: Cornell University Press.

Mather, Lynn, and Barbara Yngvesson. 1980–81. Language, Audience, and the Transformation of Disputes. *Law & Society Review* 15: 775–821.

McCann, Michael W. 1994. *Rights at Work: Pay Equity Reform and the Politics of Legal Mobilization.* Chicago: University of Chicago Press.

Mills, Anne, Sara Bennett, Porntep Siriwanarangsun, and Viroj Tangcharoensathien. 2000. The Response of Providers to Capitation Payment: A Case-Study from Thailand. *Health Policy* 51: 163–180.

Montesquieu. 1989 [1748]. *The Spirit of the Laws.* Trans. and ed. Anne M. Cohler, Basia Carolyn Miller, and Harold Samuel Stone. Cambridge, U.K.: Cambridge University Press.

Munger, Frank W. 1990. Trial Courts and Social Change: The Evolution of a Field of Study. *Law & Society Review* 24: 217–226.

Munger, Frank, ed. 2002. *Laboring below the Line: The New Ethnography of Poverty, Low-Wage Work, and Survival in the Global Economy.* New York: Russell Sage Foundation.

National Statistical Office of Thailand. 1966–1998. *Samut raingan satiti jangwat chiangmai (Statistical Reports of Changwat Chiang Mai)* [annual publication]. Bangkok: Office of the Prime Minister.

National Statistical Office of Thailand. 2000. Population and Housing Census 2000. Retrieved on August 3, 2009, from http://web.nso.go.th/pop2000/finalrep/cheingmaifn.pdf.

Neale, Frederick A. 1852. *Narrative of a Residence at the Capital of the Kingdom of Siam.* London: Office of the National Illustrated Library.

Nimmanhaemin, Prakhong. 1978. *Khwan lae kham riak khwan [The* khwan *and recalling the* khwan*].* In Prakhong Nimmanhaemin and Songsak Prangwatanakun, eds., *Lanna thai khadi [Thai case studies from Lanna],* 106–134. Chiangmai: Book Center of Chiangmai.

Nimmanhaeminda, Kraisri. 1965. "Put Vegetables into Baskets and People into Towns." In Lucien M. Hanks et al., eds., *Ethnographic Notes on Northern Thailand,* 6–9. Ithaca, NY: Southeast Asia Program, Cornell University.

Ongsakul, Sarassawadee. 2005. *History of Lan Na*. Trans. Chitraporn Tanratanakul. Chiangmai: Silkworm Press.

Peerenboom, Randall. 2004. Varieties of Rule of Law: An Introduction and Provisional Conclusion. In Randall Peerenboom, ed., *Asian Discourses of Rule of Law: Theories and Implementation of Rule of Law in Twelve Asian Countries, France and the U.S.*, 1–55. London and New York: Routledge.

Pérez-Perdomo, Rogelio, and Lawrence M. Friedman. 2003. Latin Legal Cultures in the Age of Globalization. In Lawrence M. Friedman and Rogelio Pérez-Perdomo eds., *Legal Culture in the Age of Globalization: Latin America and Latin Europe*, 1–19. Stanford, CA: Stanford University Press.

Petchsiri, Apirat. 1987. *Eastern Importation of Western Criminal Law: Thailand as a Case Study*. Littleton, CO: Fred B. Rothman & Co.

Phongpaichit, Pasuk, and Chris Baker. 1998. *Thailand's Boom and Bust*. Chiangmai: Silkworm Press.

Rajadhon, Phaya Anuman [pseudonym Sathian Koset]. 1963. *Khwan lae prapheni kan tham khwan* [*The* khwan *and ceremonies for the* khwan]. Bangkok: Kaaw Naa Press.

Ramitanon, Shalardchai. 2002. *Phi jao nai [Spirits of the nobility]*, 2nd ed. Chiangmai: Ming Mŭang Press.

Ramsay, James Ansil. 1971. *The Development of a Bureaucratic Polity: The Case of Northern Siam*. Unpublished Ph.D. dissertation, Cornell University.

Reynolds, Frank. 1994. Dhamma in Dispute: The Interaction of Religion and Law in Thailand. *Law & Society Review* 28: 433–51.

Rhum, Michael R. 1994. *The Ancestral Lords: Gender, Descent, and Spirits in a Northern Thai Village*. Special Report No. 29, Monograph Series on Southeast Asia. DeKalb: Center for Southeast Asian Studies, Northern Illinois University.

Robertson, Roland. 1992. *Globalization: Social Theory and Global Culture*. London: Sage Publications.

Rosen, Lawrence. 2006. *Law as Culture: An Invitation*. Princeton, NJ: Princeton University Press.

Saks, Michael J. 1992. Do We Really Know Anything about the Behavior of the Tort Litigation System—and Why Not? *University of Pennsylvania Law Review* 140: 1147–1292.

Santos, Boaventura de Sousa. 1995. *Toward a New Common Sense: Law, Science and Politics in the Paradigmatic Transition*. New York: Routledge.

Sarat, Austin and Thomas R. Kearns. 1995. Beyond the Great Divide: Forms of Legal Scholarship and Everyday Life. In Austin Sarat and Thomas R. Kearns, eds., *Law in Everyday Life*, 21–61. Ann Arbor: University of Michigan Press.

Sassen, Saskia. 2001. Spatialities and Temporalities of the Global: Elements for a Theorization. In Arjun Appadurai, ed., *Globalization*, 260–278. Durham, NC: Duke University Press.

Scott, James C. 1998. *Seeing Like a State: How Certain Schemes to Improve the Human Condition Have Failed*. New Haven, CT: Yale University Press.

Shamir, Ronen. 2004. Between Self-Regulation and the Alien Tort Claims Act: On the Contested Concept of Corporate Social Responsibility. *Law & Society Review* 38: 635–64.

Sivaraksa, Sulak. 1992. *Seeds of Peace: A Buddhist Vision for Renewing Society.* Berkeley, CA: Parallax Press.

Stephens, Beth. 2002. Translating Filártiga: A Comparative and International Law Analysis of Domestic Remedies for International Human Rights Violations. *Yale Journal of International Law* 27: 1–58.

Supakankunti, Siripen. 2000. Future Prospects of Voluntary Health Insurance in Thailand. *Health Policy and Planning* 15: 85–94.

Supphanit, Susom. 1994. *Laksana lamoet [The law of torts].* Bangkok: Nitibannagarn.

Swearer, Donald K., Sommai Premchit, and Phaithoon Dokbuakaew. 2004. *Sacred Mountains of Northern Thailand and Their Legends.* Chiangmai: Silkworm Press.

Tambiah, S. J. 1970. *Buddhism and the Spirit Cults in North-East Thailand.* London: Cambridge University Press.

Tambiah, S. J. 1976. *World Conqueror and World Renouncer: A Study of Buddhism and Polity in Thailand against a Historical Background.* Cambridge, U.K.: Cambridge University Press.

Tanabe, Shigeharu. 2002. The Person in Transformation: Body, Mind and Cultural Appropriation. In Shigeharu Tanabe and Charles F. Keyes, eds., *Cultural Crisis and Social Memory: Modernity and Identity in Thailand and Laos,* 43–67. Honolulu: University of Hawaii Press.

Tanase, Takao. 1990. The Management of Disputes: Automobile Accident Compensation in Japan. *Law & Society Review* 24: 651–691.

Tangcharoensathien, Viroj, Samrit Srithamrongsawat, and Siriwan Pitayarangsarit. 2004a. Overview of Health Insurance Systems in Thailand. In World Health Organization, ed., *Regional Overview of Social Health Insurance in South-East Asia,* 175–189. New Delhi: Regional Office for South-East Asia.

Tangcharoensathien, Viroj, Anuwat Supachutikul, and Jongkol Lertiendumrong. 1999. The Social Security Scheme in Thailand: What Lessons Can Be Drawn? *Social Science & Medicine* 48: 913–923.

Tangcharoensathien, Viroj, Suwit Wibulpholprasert, and Sanguan Nitayaramphong. 2004b. Knowledge-Based Changes to Health Systems: The Thai Experience in Policy Development. *Bulletin of the World Health Organization* 82: 750–756.

Terwiel, B. J. 1976. Leasing from the Gods (Thailand). *Anthropos* 71: 254–274.

Toharia, Jose Juan. 1976. Economic Development and Litigation: The Case of Spain. *Jahrbuch fur Rechtssoziologie und Rechtstheorie* 4: 39–42.

Towse, Adrian, Anne Mills, and Viroj Tangcharoensathien. 2004. Learning from Thailand's Health Reforms. *BMJ* 328: 103–105.

Trubek, David M., Austin Sarat, William L. F. Felstiner, Herbert M. Kritzer, and Joel B. Grossman. 1983. The Costs of Ordinary Litigation. *UCLA Law Review* 31: 73–129.

Tsing, Anna. 2000. Conclusion: The Global Situation. In Jonathan Xavier Inda and Renato Rosaldo, eds., *The Anthropology of Globalization: A Reader*, 453–485. Blackwell Publishers: Malden, MA.

United Nations Development Programme (UNDP). 2003. *Thailand Human Development Report 2003 on Community Empowerment and Human Development*. Bangkok, Thailand: United Nations Development Programme.

U.S. Census Bureau. 2009. American FactFinder. Retrieved on August 1, 2009, from: http://factfinder.census.gov/home/saff/main.html?_lang=en.

Vickery, Michael. 1970. Thai Regional Elites and the Reforms of King Chulalongkorn. *Journal of Asian Studies* 29: 863–881.

Wannasaeng, Phattharasak. 1995. *Yo laksana lamoet [Overview of the law of torts]*. Bangkok: Nititham Publishing House.

Weber, Max. 1978. *Economy and Society: An Outline of Interpretive Sociology*. Guenther Roth and Claus Wittich, eds. Berkeley: University of California Press.

Wijeyewardene, Gehan. 1970. The Still Point and the Turning World: Towards the Structure of Northern Thai Religion. *Mankind* 7: 247–255.

Winichakul, Thongchai. 1994. *Siam Mapped: A History of the Geo-Body of a Nation*. Honolulu: University of Hawaii Press.

World Health Organization (WHO). 2003. *Social Health Insurance: Report of a Regional Consultation, Bangkok, Thailand, 7–9 July 2003*. New Delhi: Regional Office for South-East Asia.

Wyatt, David K. 1984. *Thailand: A Short History*. New Haven, CT: Yale University Press.

Yŭ, Chŭn-fang. 2001. *Kuan-yin: The Chinese Transformation of Avalokiteśvara*. New York: Columbia University Press.

Thai Laws, Law Codes, and Treaties

Charter of the Courts of Justice. 1935.

Civil and Commercial Code. 1935.

Civil Procedure Code. 1935.

Criminal Procedure Code. 1935.

Law of the Courts of Justice. 1908. Sathian Laiyalak et al., comps., *Prachum kotmai prajam sok* vol. 22: 238. Bangkok: Daily Mail, 19351953.

Law of Evidence. 1895. Sathian Laiyalak et al., comps., *Prachum kotmai prajam sok* vol. 14: 225. Bangkok: Daily Mail, 1935–1953.

Law of the Provincial Courts. 1896. Sathian Laiyalak et al., comps., *Prachum kotmai prajam sok* vol. 15: 54. Bangkok: Daily Mail, 1935–1953.

Penal Code. 1908. Sathian Laiyalak et al., comps., *Prachum kotmai prajam sok* vol. 22:1. Bangkok: Daily Mail, 1935–1953.

Products Liability Law. 2008.

Provisional Code of Civil Procedure. 1896. Sathian Laiyalak et al., comps., *Prachum kotmai prajam sok* vol. 15:157. Bangkok: Daily Mail, 1935–1953.

Provisional Code of Criminal Procedure. 1896. Sathian Laiyalak et al., comps., *Prachum kotmai prajam sok* vol. 15: 106. Bangkok: Daily Mail, 1935–1953.

Royal Edict Concerning Persons Injured by Vehicles. 1992.

Treaty between Great Britain and Siam for Promoting Commercial Intercourse between British Burma and Adjoining Territories Belonging to Siam, signed at Calcutta. 1874. 66 B.S.P. 537; 147 Consol. T.S. 187.

Treaty between Great Britain and Siam for the Prevention of Crime in Chiengmai etc., signed at Bangkok. 1883. 74 B.S.P. 78; 162 Consol. T.S. 377.

Index

Note: Page numbers in italic type indicate illustrations, figures, or tables.

THE CULTURAL LIVES OF LAW
Austin Sarat, Editor

The Cultural Lives of Law series brings insights and approaches from cultural studies to law and tries to secure for law a place in cultural analysis. Books in the series focus on the production, interpretation, consumption, and circulation of legal meanings. They take up the challenges posed as boundaries collapse between as well as within cultures and as the circulation of legal meanings becomes more fluid. They also attend to the ways law's power in cultural production is renewed and resisted.
